BORDELLOS OF BLAIR STREET

*The story of Silverton, Colorado's
Notorious Red Light District*

**Revised Edition
By Allan G. Bird**

Published by
Advertising, Publications & Consultants
4444 Bass Lake Rd.
Pierson, Michigan 49339

ISBN 0-9619382-1-8

COVER: A Durango prostitute taken about 1920.
Andy Hanahan Photo.

PRINTED IN THE UNITED STATES OF AMERICA

DEDICATION

I wish to dedicate this book to - - - - - Hell, nobody wants this book dedicated to them.

ACKNOWLEDGMENT

Many thanks to the fine people of Silverton who took the time to share their memories and photos. I wish to express my thanks to Jim and Marge Bell, Andy Hanahan, Fritz Klinke, Lou Parcell, Fiore Giacomelli, Julia Maffey, Nona Salfisberg, "Corky" Scheer, Annie Smith, Lena and Herman Dalla, John and Joe Matties, "Leach" Zanoni, Jim Hook, Sr., Mary and Gerald Swanson, Tom Savich, the late Eddie Lorenzon, Ernest Hoffman and James Cole Sr., and the San Juan County Historical Society. Many of the above have passed on since the first edition of this book in 1987.

THE AUTHOR

Allan G. Bird is a graduate mining geologist. He holds a Bachelor of Science degree from the University of Illinois and a Master of Science degree from the University of Colorado. Between May of 1971 and September of 1977, he was the general manager of Silverton's Sunnyside Mine, Colorado's largest underground gold mine. It was during this time that he developed a love for the San Juans and the people of Silverton.

In May of 1986 he published his first book entitled "Silverton Gold," the story of the Sunnyside Mine. He received excellent press reviews and his first edition was sold out within a year. The first edition of Bordellos of Blair Street was published in 1987. In 1990, he published his last book entitled "Silverton-Then & Now." At the present time, he has his own consulting business and lives with his wife Norma at Lakewood, Colorado.

FOREWARD

By 1910, the last large bordellos had been built in Silverton. From that date forward, the buildings continued to be occupied by either saloons, boarding houses or bordellos. The one exception was the Arcade Saloon, now the Arcade Gift Shop. This building was constructed in 1929. Whether or not a building housed prostitutes depended upon the owner at the time. Some of the boarding houses were family-run enterprises and catered only to miners. The previous owner of the same building may have used the premises for a dance hall and bordello.

During the 1920's, in the era of Prohibition, Silverton's Blair Street was, in the words of an old timer, "Like a little Las Vegas, the gambling houses and bordellos were open 24 hours a day, seven days a week. You could buy bootleg booze in any saloon or whorehouse."

One of the dangers in writing about the subject of "bordellos" is the reluctance of those still living to admit that grandma was a Madame. In several cases, relatives have stated that grandma or grandpa ran only a saloon and boarding house. When photos of their old buildings were shown to one "old timer" over 85 years of age, her immediate reply was "Why that was the biggest "hook-shop" in Silverton. Mrs._____ once told me she had 35 girls working for her at one time."

The book is not a condemnation of the women who worked on the "line." It is an attempt to preserve, for the record, a part of the American frontier that existed but is now history. Ethnic terms, that today would be totally unacceptable, were commonplace. Names such as "Nigger" Lola, "Jew" Fanny, "Sheeny" Pearl, were not only tolerated, they were accepted as "trade marks" by the women themselves.

During the late 1930's, in the midst of the Great Depression, Nona Salfisberg, who was a young hairdresser at the time, recalled that there were only about sixteen girls left on the "line." She was frequently called upon to do their hair.

Prostitution and gambling existed in Silverton until the late 1940's. The exact date of the exit of the last prostitute, "Jew" Fanny, is questionable. The most authoratative sources say she left in 1948.

The various houses will be discussed in the following chapters, using the final name of the establishment. For example, the "Laundry" was the colorful name given to Jack Gilheany's gambling hall and bordello. This building was built by Jane Bowen in 1880, later operated by Joe Satore and Ludwig Vota, followed by Billy Luke, and finally by Jack Gilheany.

The author found numerous conflicts of memory in the many people interviewed. Errors may exist in the names and locations of some of the more obscure establishments. One person would say, "this building was the Green Lantern," while others could not remember of ever hearing such a name.

ALLAN G. BIRD

TABLE OF CONTENTS

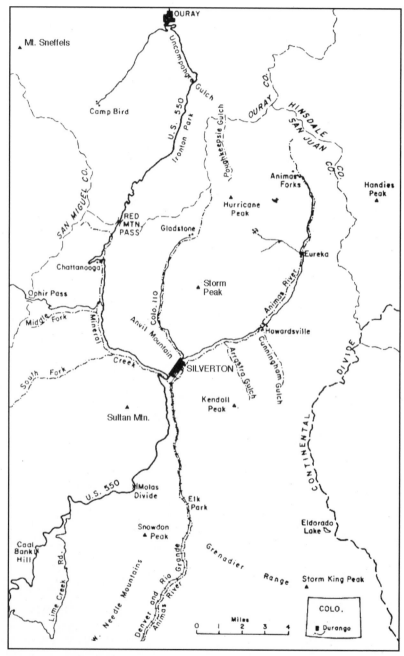

Fig 1   Index Map of San Juan County - - 1987.

BORDELLOS OF BLAIR STREET

SILVERTON, COLORADO

CHAPTER ONE

THE BEGINNING

It was Christmas Eve, 1974, one hundred years from Silverton's first Christmas Eve. The temperature was hovering near minus-ten degrees below zero. The town was silent except for the crunch of frozen snow underfoot. Ice crystals drifted lazily from a crisp cold sky. As I strolled through town that cold winter evening, I yearned for a time machine to turn back the clock to the days when Silverton's streets were lined with saloons, dance halls, variety theaters, and the ever-present bordellos. Days, when just-paid boisterous miners reveled throughout the night, relieving the boredom of long months in the mine boarding houses. During those boom years, silence was a commodity yearned for but seldom found. Perhaps the most vivid description of those times was reported in the _Silverton Democrat_ of November 22, 1884. They printed an article entitled "Life, Labor, and Lotteries in High Altitudes." The article read:

Silverton, Colorado, November 2,——There are 27 saloons in this mining camp, nine of them in the block opposite the hotel (Grand Imperial). In one a man is continually yelling out the numbers of the "Wheel of Fortune" in a noise that counterfeits the music of a tin pan and stove lifter. At night the uproar is hideous. A loud piano in one den runs through three charming chords, drowning a vilely squeaking fiddle from seven in the evening until sleep has mercifully closed one's ears. Farther down the block is heard the singing of a woman whose voice is much too good for the surroundings, for there are Faro tables in all of these holes. The betting and drinking are pretty heavy when the miners are freshly paid up; and they revel in a beer at 15 cents a glass or two for a quarter, and get much foam and glass for the money.

CHAPTER ONE

Sunday is not generally observed save by increased guzzling. There is a Congregational 'Church edifice' here, sparsely attended and an occasional Roman Catholic service, but if any zealous missionary is burning to enlighten and convert the heathen he could get a good deal of practice here.

Silverton swarms with dogs who invade the hotel halls and decorously come to their meals with their masters. They contribute to the general amusements by improvising a fight, Marquis of Dogberry rules, and as many rounds as possible about every hour of the day. Like the contests in Madison Square Arena, these attract large audiences, biped and quadruped. A grizzled old fellow, a victim of bilious seductions named, I often see reeling along among his fine enormous dogs, a pitiful contrast to their grave sobriety.

Greene Street, the main street of Silverton named after George Greene, an early day merchant and smelter builder, was lined with saloons having colorful names such as: The Rose Bud, Westminster Hall, Arion, The Crystal Palace, Johnnie Goode's, The Fashion, The Arlington, (where Wyatt Earp managed the gambling rooms in 1883) and Tom Blair's Assembly Rooms, to name a few. One block to the east lies Blair Street,[1] named after Tom Blair, one of the original pioneers who entered the valley of the upper Animas in 1871 searching for gold. To the west (northwest) of Greene Street lies Reese Street, followed by Snowden Avenue.[2] Reese, Blair and Snowden formed the Silverton Town Company and were responsible for laying out the town plat. The town was divided into rectangular blocks 300 feet long, each divided into twenty-four lots 25 X 100 feet in size. Each block was divided by an alley with twelve lots on either side of the alley.

---

[1] Blair Street is actually to the southeast of Green Street. Silverton's main streets trend northeast and the cross streets southeast and northwest.

[2] Named for Dempsey Reese and Col. Francis M. Snowden who, along with Blair, entered what was then known as Baker's Park. Snowden built the first log cabin in what is today Silverton.

2

THE BEGINNING

Silverton was originally known as Baker's Park, named after the discoverer Charles Baker, who entered the San Juan Mountains in the late summer and early fall of 1860. The November 15, 1883, _San Juan Herald_ printed a letter from one of the original members of the Baker Party. It read:

> There were 150 men in the original 1860 Baker Party. They reached Baker's Park in September and prospected about three weeks. The party scattered. Since then nothing definite has been heard from more than twelve of the old original Baker Party. (Signed) Frank Koerle, member of original party.

Many of the group probably froze to death or were killed by Indians; however, little actually is known of their fate. Baker was killed by Indians several years later. Their prospecting expedition was considered a failure. Only small amounts of gold were found near the present townsite of Eureka, about seven miles north of Silverton. The Civil War broke out the following year. Prospecting was put aside until 1871 when George Howard, a member of the original Baker Party, organized a group of men at Del Norte, Colorado and entered the San Juans in the spring of 1871. Learning from his tragic experiences of the 1860 expedition, Howard led his group out of the area each winter until the winter of 1874. By this time, many of the major mineral discoveries had been made and the Ute Indians had signed away their ownership of the land in the Brunot Treaty of September 1873. Cabins were built and a few hardy souls spent their first winter in Baker's Park. After the discovery of rich silver veins, the town's name was changed to Silverton. Some say the name is derived from the statement that "we have silver by the ton"; however, this may or may not be the case.

During the period between 1874 and 1879, the town was relatively quiet with only a few hundred residents and itinerant prospectors. There was little crime. The men who came to this difficult country came here to find gold and, for the most part, were honest, hard-working men. The April 12, 1879, _La Plata Miner_ summarized the condition of the town in its article entitled "Compliment to an Efficient Officer." It read as follows:

No more deserving and worthy compliment could have been paid to Mr. James Cart, who has been the efficient marshal of Silverton for the past year, than that which he received at the polls on Monday last, being no less than the unanimous endorsement of the people of Silverton for the same position for the ensuing year. There was not a single vote against him. Our town during the past summer was remarkably orderly for a mining camp, especially for the business center of the mining districts of southern Colorado and San Juan. The reelection of Mr. Cart is a guarantee of order and respect for the law the coming summer.

As early as 1874, men were bringing their wives and families into Silverton. This provided an incentive to keep, at least part of the town, respectable. From the very beginning there was an imaginary dividing line between the good, church-going people and the gamblers and prostitutes. At first this line passed down the center of Greene Street. The east side of the street, across the street from the present Grand Imperial Hotel, was known as the "liquor side of Greene Street." The earliest brothels were built on Blair Street; however, their numbers were few as late as 1883. Most of the women worked in dance halls. During these early years there is no record of how many there were or how they operated. The town ordinances of 1879 recognized the problem and made it clear what the penalties for gambling and prostitution would be. They read as follows:

1879 TOWN ORDINANCES

Author's Note: A liquor license costs $200.

Sec. 3. Any person who shall keep a bawdy house, house of ill fame or assignation or shall knowingly lease or permit property in his possession or under his control to be used for any such purpose, shall be declared guilty of a misdemeanor and upon conviction be fined not less than $50 nor more than $300.

Sec. 4. Any prostitute who shall be an inmate of any such house mentioned in the last proceeding section, for the purpose of prostitution or who shall commit acts of prostitution in any place in this town shall be deemed guilty of a misdemeanor and upon conviction be fined not less than ten nor more than $100.

THE BEGINNING

Sec. 5. Any keeper of a draw shop, beer house, ale house, saloon, hotel or other place of public resort who shall employ a lewd woman or any woman having the reputation of a prostitute as a carrier of beer or any other article or to sing or dance in a lewd or indecent manner or permit any such lewd woman to act as bartender in any such house or place shall be guilty of a misdemeanor and upon conviction be fined not less than $70 nor more than $100.

Sec. 6. Any person who shall keep in this town a house where lewd or disorderly persons assemble for dancing shall be guilty of a misdemeanor and upon conviction be fined not less than $50 nor more than $200.

*after the fine was paid
it was business as usual*

Sec. 7. Any person who shall keep a gambling house in this town or set up or keep any gaming table or gambling device at which any game of chance shall be played for money or property or any thing representing money or shall at any such table or device or at any game of chance bet, win or lose, any money or property—either in specie or by means of any thing representing the same or shall suffer any such table or device at which any game of chance is played, shall be guilty of a misdemeanor and upon conviction be fined not less than $25 nor more than $300.

The town fathers spoke out loud and clear against gambling and prostitution. What happened? It seems that once laws are on the books it takes enforcement to make them stick. This is where Silverton's good intentions broke down. For the most part, it took tough men to keep law and order in a frontier town full of rowdy miners. The toughest men were the saloon and dance hall owners. With very few exceptions, Silverton's early lawmen were either owners of saloons and dance halls or were sympathetic to their existence. Rather than close these vice dens, they did what was socially acceptable, they periodically arrested the owners and the girls. A monthly fine was imposed to help defray the cost of city government. After the fine was paid, it was business as usual.

CHAPTER TWO
EARLY BLAIR STREET

During the early history of Silverton, Blair Street began to evolve as the red light district; however, its development did not really get started until about 1878. The oldest recorded whorehouse was purchased by Alice Morris on September 16, 1878.[3]

Oldest Bordello

Blair Street

Fig. 2 1883 Photo Showing Blair Street's oldest bordello, built in 1877. Colo. Hist. Soc. Photo.

ALICE MORRIS AND ALICE HANKE

The small frame house was built by Joseph Wallace in late 1877 or early 1878. Wallace sold the building and lot for $500 to Elmer King on July 17, 1878. Nine days after he purchased the house, King sold the property to George Walz for $500. Walz gave a warranty deed to Ernest Stephan, Jr. on July 23rd, three days before King recorded the sale to him. Ernest Stephan, Jr. sold the house to Alice Morris. Alice ran the house until October 8, 1880, when she sold it to Alice Hanke.

Fig. 3   Present site of Blair Street's oldest bordello, now occupied by the Olde Time Photography Gallery. Front half of building includes original 1877 building. Rear portion moved from ghost town of Middleton. Allan Bird Photo.

THE "SAGE HEN"

Jane Bowen, known as the "Sage Hen," and her husband William arrived in Silverton as early as 1875. Jane came here from London, England. Their initial interest was in mining. William Bowen made an agreement on August 25, 1875, with a Dwight Haywood to enter into an equal partnership which would entitle Bowen to half interest in all claims staked by Haywood since December 13, 1873. Jane managed the first variety show ever performed in Silverton in 1875. On September 18, 1876, Bowen bought a lot on the northeast corner of 12th and Greene Streets from Dempsey Reese.[5] He constructed a false-front frame building on the lot and opened a saloon and dance hall-bordello which he named Westminster Hall after his wife's home in London. The miners called it the "Sage Hen's" Dance Hall. On July 6, 1880, Jane Bowen purchased a lot on the northwest corner of 12th and Blair streets, directly behind Westminster Hall. She immediately began construction of the her new residence. The structure was large by early Silverton Standards. The front occupied the entire 25 foot width of the lot and the building was about 60 feet deep. The type

7

of architecture was simple, similar to a World War II army barracks.[4] In 1884, Silverton passed an ordinance against prostitution on Greene Street and the building was enlarged to a length of 80 feet and converted into a bordello-dance hall to replace their lucrative business in Westminster Hall. Jane and her husband continued to occupy a portion of the building as a residence.

Fig. 4   Late 1883 photo showing Blair Street buildings on block between 12th and 13th streets. Looking toward the west. Colo. Hist. Soc. Photo.

William Bowen was one of the largest taxpayers in San Juan County. His assessed valuation in 1875 was $740. Five hundred was for merchandise and $240 for twelve asses. By 1876 William Bowen was the sixth highest taxpayer in the county, assessed $950. The largest taxpayer was George Greene & Co., assessed $7715; followed by Greene Eberhart & Co. assessed $7700. Greene owned the new smelter and Greene Eberhart & Co. operated the first general merchandise store in early Silverton.

In 1880, William Bowen's health began to fail, he was afflicted with miners consumption. He deeded all of his property to his wife Jane. The Bowens did not have any children of their own; however, they did have an adopted daughter who would have been about eleven years old in 1880. The new residence was completed in late October or early November of 1880. The lumber company that sold Jane the lumber and shingles filed a lien against the property in October of 1880 for unpaid supplies. The lien was later paid.

EARLY BLAIR STREET

In June of 1881, Jane purchased the Poorman Mine on Sultan Mountain from John McKenna for $10,000 cash. This was a fortune at that time. The Bowens were, by early standards, quite wealthy.

By the end of 1880, Blair Street had only five buildings in the two blocks between 11th and 13th streets, later to become the core of the red light district. The tax rolls show that a Mrs. Alice Hanke owned the small house previously mentioned. This was the only building on the block in 1880. The next block to the north, between 12th and 13th Streets, had four buildings (three on the west side of the street and one on the east side); Jane Bowen's on the corner, Alice Norris' next door, and on the southwest corner of 13th and Blair streets, Mary Scheidt's. Alice Norris' place was a typical early-day bordello, probably with a small saloon and three or four small rooms. Mary Scheidt owned the two corner lots, just to the north of the present Swanee's Gift Shop. Her small house was on the corner lot. Nothing is known of her except that she was married to a shoemaker and had a child in the mid-1890's. Her home was an early residence and not a bordello.

Across the street, three lots north of 12th Street, was an unknown building owned by a G. T. Stauton who sold it to a Mrs. Ellen Murry for $1000 on September 14, 1880. This building actually predated Jane Bowen's by a few months. By 1885, the assessment on Mrs. Murry's lot was only $300. The sudden drop in value would indicate that the 1880 building was probably destroyed by fire and a small crib built in its place.

CITY JAIL

Blair Street was rapidly gaining the reputation of being a rough area early in the history of Silverton. The January 15, 1881, issue of the *La Plata Miner* wrote:

> There was an affray in the vicinity of Blair Street last Sunday night in which a Durangoite received some serious injuries about the head. Results attributed to overdose of Pendleton's rheumatic remedy. Receipt to the town treasury $40.

CHAPTER TWO

Pendleton was an early saloon keeper in Silverton.

The town fathers decided early in the history of Silverton to locate their civic buildings on Blair Street. They built the new city hall in 1883 on the west side of Blair between 12th and 13th streets. Remnants of this building still remain. The first jail was built in 1875 on the west side of Blair a few lots south of 14th Street. The original building was of log construction and was placed on the lot at an angle, for reasons unknown. By July 1881, the _La Plata Miner_ had this to say:

> Silverton, although the boss town of the Rockies, is lamentably deficient in its 'jail accommodations.' Our village lockup is simply a disgrace, and would compare favorably with a second-class pig stye. A movement should be made to build a new one in a different location.

Perhaps the low point in Silverton's history occurred in 1881 in this jail. Burt Wilkinson, Dyson Eskridge, and a black man by the name of Brown were part of the Ike Stockton gang. These gentlemen could be described as Durango's badmen. For the most part, they concentrated on rustling cattle in northern New Mexico and selling them in Durango and Animas City. In April 1881, the New Mexican law officers organized a posse and intercepted the Stockton gang on a rustling raid. A heated gun battle broke out in which dozens of shots were fired by both sides. Only two men were slightly wounded and Stockton and his gang retreated to Colorado. After this encounter, Stockton concentrated on robbing stage-coaches and isolated travelers in Colorado. Their headquarters alternated between Rico and Durango. Wilkinson, Eskridge and Brown decided to go on a drinking spree in Silverton, where they were relatively unknown. Word reached the Silverton law officers of their arrival and soon Sheriff Luke Hunter of La Plata County arrived. He talked Marshal Ogsbury into trying to apprehend the gang without help.

The August 25, 1881, _San Juan Herald_ printed the following story of the murder of town marshal D. C. Ogsbury:

EARLY BLAIR STREET

MIDNIGHT MURDER

Our City Marshal D. C. Ogsbury Shot Down Last Evening
by Burt Wilkinson

Last night turned out to be one of the most sad and bloody ones in the history of Silverton. Our good marshal D. C. Ogsbury was shot down in cold blood by the desperado Burt Wilkinson on the outside of the Diamond Saloon. The facts, as well as we can abbreviate them, are as follows:

It was known early last evening that Wilkinson, Eskridge and others of the gang had arrived in town during the day. It is also well known that rewards are out from La Plata county for their arrest and capture and that parties from below were on their track.

Mr. C. W. Hodges, who arrived back from Durango about 5:30 brought in word that the gang had passed him on the road below Rico House and he notified the officers here of their presence in Silverton. Our sheriff and marshal would have arrested them at once before dark had they received the warrants from La Plata county to do so. They waited until the mail from Durango arrived, and as it brought no orders they dropped the matter for the night, and in due time retired to bed.

At about 11 o'clock the Sheriff of La Plata county, Luke Hunter, arrived in town with the warrants etc., for the arrest of Eskridge and Wilkinson, and waking up Mr. Hodges, repaired to Marshal Ogsbury's room, at the rear of Goode's Saloon, and woke him up and got him out, told him the circumstances and the object of the sheriff's visit to Silverton, and that the desperadoes were at the time somewhere in or about the Diamond Saloon. Ogsbury said if they were going to arrest the parties they should have more help. But the La Plata Sheriff appeared to think not and our marshal did not insist: and so, in company with Mr. Hodges, Ogsbury and Hunter walked down to the saloon together, and just as they arrived near the door, Ogsbury observed someone leaning against the outside of the saloon in the shadow, and putting his head forward and peering into the darkness to see who it might be, and just as he saw it was Wilkinson, before the marshal had an opportunity to say a word or put his hand on his revolver, Wilkinson drew his gun and shot Ogsbury, killing him almost instantly. The marshal fell on his face, and when Mr. Hodges asked him if he was hurt, he uttered only a groan. Hodges turned him over on his back, and at the same time the bullets were whistling by him on every side, and seeing he could do Ogsbury no good, and that his own life was in danger, he retired across the street, and waited till the firing was over. He judges that about twelve shots were fired.

CHAPTER TWO

When the firing ceased, some one of the gang called the roll, and without attempting to take their horses, which were at Carlisle's Livery Stable, they decamped on foot. Hodges then went over and found Ogsbury just gasping his last breath. He tried to get some help in the dance hall, but could not as they were having a general row in there, but about that time Hiram Herr and another man came along having returned from a run down toward the tollgate, and the three carried the body of the unfortunate Ogsbury to Johnnie Goode's Saloon. In the meantime several parties of horsemen had been organized, starting in all directions to scour the country and get on the trail of the desperadoes if possible. Fortunately the telephone line was open to Lake City, and dispatches were at once forwarded to that point, Alamosa, Durango, and in every possible direction. Our fire bell was rung and the alarm given far and near.

After Ogsbury's murder, the gang made a break for the hills, leaving their horses in Silverton. Brown, known as the "Copper Colored Kid," was captured in the city limits of Silverton and lynched by a Silverton mob the following night. Wilkinson and Eskridge escaped to the Castle Rock Stage Station, about fifteen or twenty miles north of Durango, where they were hidden and fed by the wife of the station manager. Word was sent to Stockton at Durango that the two needed horses and supplies. Stockton had already heard of the $2500 reward being offered for the capture of either man. He proceeded to the stage station and told Dyson Eskridge to go to a ranch on the Pine River and get some horses. Eskridge was the larger and stronger of the two men; Stockton knew he could handle Wilkinson but not both men. Eskridge followed Stockton's instructions and as soon as he was out of earshot, Stockton pulled a gun on Wilkinson and informed him that he was his prisoner and that he was turning him in for the reward. He took Wilkinson to Animas City were he tied him up and locked him in a stone barn. He then contacted the law officers at Silverton, and informed them that he had their man. He wanted assurances that he would not personally be harmed, and that the reward would be paid. Stockton was squeamish about entering Silverton with Wilkinson for fear that the mob would lynch them both. He told the Silverton authorities that Eskridge had escaped and he had no idea where he was headed. Sheriff Thorniley, of San Juan County, wired Stockton giving him his personal guarantee that he would not be harmed and that the reward would be paid.

Arrangements were made for Deputy Marshal Cook of La Plata County, Mayor Fox of Durango, and a Mr. Hull to meet Stockton and Wilkinson and escort the two men to the San Juan County line. There, Sheriff Thorniley and a posse of twelve men would meet the two and escort them to Silverton. Stockton and Wilkinson were taken to the bank for payment of the reward. The posse took Wilkinson and placed him in the small log jail on Blair Street. A heavy armed guard was placed around the jail. Stockton was taken in the bank and paid the $2500 reward in gold coin. Since it was late, Stockton was escorted to one of Silverton's early hotels, the Walker House, for the night. Stockton spent a restless night but was pleasantly surprised when he was given an armed escort out of town with the reward money in his pockets. Stockton should have known that he had just signed his own death warrant. Until this time he had been on more-or-less friendly terms with the local law officers of Durango. Jim Sullivan, the deputy sheriff was a personal friend. When word reach Durango that Stockton had turned in his friend for the reward, there wasn't a man in Durango that didn't want to see Stockton dead.

Wilkinson expected no mercy from the people of Silverton and had resigned himself to his fate. He admitted that he had intended to kill someone, hopefully, Sheriff Hunter of La Plata County. His only defense was that Eskridge was equally to blame. He said that both were firing simultaneously and he could not be certain who killed Ogsbury. He was allowed no visitors while in jail. His sister and brother-in-law arrived early Sunday to plead with the local officials for a fair trial. Wilkinson was a little surprised that he was still alive. He fully expected to be hung by the mob the previous night. He was taken by the sheriff to the local photographer to pose for a last photograph. No copies of this photo have ever been found. Wilkinson's sister and brother-in-law left for Durango in the afternoon, dejected and certain that the sentence had already been passed.

Wilkinson asked only that he be allowed to shoot Stockton before his execution. He begged that Stockton be placed in his cell for a short time and then he would gladly help the mob put the rope around his neck. This last wish was denied. The September 8, 1881, issue of the *San Juan Herald* printed a detailed description of Wilkinson's last moments on earth:

OGSBURY'S MURDERER NO MORE

Between nine and ten Sunday evening, just at a time when the town was usually quiet, when but few people were on the street, and apparently nothing unusual transpiring, a party of masked men suddenly appeared before the guards at the jail and overpowered both of them and the jailer, went into the jail and seizing Wilkinson, passed the noose about his neck and asked him if he had anything to say before his death. He replied: 'Nothing, gentlemen, adios!' He was perfectly composed to the very last, got up on a chair and assisted the vigilantes to hasten the hanging. The chair was removed, and he dropped, dying in a short time without hardly a struggle. The body was found in his cell suspended in the manner above described, and the coroner was at once notified.

This ends the second act of the great tragedy of avenging Marshal Ogsbury's cruel death, and as we predicted hardly a week since, summary justice has been dealt out to the ruthless murderer of one of our best beloved and respected citizens. There was no disturbance of any kind. The people expected the result recorded above, and Wilkinson expected it. This young man, steeped in crime before he had reached manhood's legal estate, and ending his career in this ignominious way should be a warning to the outlaws and desperadoes throughout the State.

Silverton does nothing by halves. Her people started out for justice and spared neither expense or vigilance and the result is that Wilkinson has met his just deserts. Now for Eskridge.

Ike Stockton was soon to follow Wilkinson to that promised land. He had committed the unforgivable sin of turning in a friend for the reward. This placed him on the most wanted list of both outlaw and lawmen. Deputy Sheriff Jim Sullivan knew that Stockton had outstanding warrants for his arrest in Texas. He obtained a warrant from the law officers of Gainesville, Texas and proceeded to search for Stockton. He knew that Stockton would not be taken without a fight. In late September 1881, Sullivan met Stockton on the sidewalks of Durango. He pulled his gun in one hand and the warrant in the other. As he started to hand the warrant to Stockton, Ike went for his gun. Before he could level the gun, Sullivan fired, hitting him in the leg. The bullet shattered the upper leg bone and cut the femoral artery. Stockton fired one shot into the sidewalk and collapsed. He was carried to the office of the local Durango smelter and allowed to bleed to death. The hatred of Stockton was so great that no one would go for a doctor. He died friendless, and was buried in the old Animas City Cemetery. His tombstone was seen by the author in the 1970's, lying on the ground removed from his grave. He was only twenty-nine years old.

The murder of Ogsbury took place on Greene Street. The Diamond Saloon was located on the southeast corner of 11th and Greene Streets. At the time, it was the first saloon on Greene Street as you entered town from the south. It was also a bordello operated by a gal with the delicate name of Bronco Lou. Lou was jailed about three days prior to the shooting for slipping knockout drops in a miner's drink and robbing him of approximately $350. Goode's saloon was on the southeast corner of 13th and Greene streets.[6]

Fig. 5   Late July 1883 photo showing location of Goode's Saloon and the Diamond Saloon where Burt Wilkinson murdered Marshal Ogsbury in 1881. Colo. Hist. Soc. Photo.

The old jail in which Wilkinson was lynched was later rotated about forty-five degrees so that it was square with the lot. In later years, a home was built around the structure. It wasn't until the late 1970's that its location was rediscovered after a fire damaged the house. The bars of this jail are now in the San Juan County Historical Society Museum in Silverton. The building has been demolished.

---

3   This building is located on the west side of Blair Street between 11th and 12th streets directly across the street from the present Bent Elbow Restaurant.

4   The present site of the High Noon Hamburger stand across the street from where the train stops.

5   This is the corner lot now occupied by the Benson building directly across Greene Street from the Grand Imperial Hotel.

6   On the corner lot directly across the street, to the south, of the present day Pickle Barrel Restaurant.

CHAPTER THREE
GREENE STREET

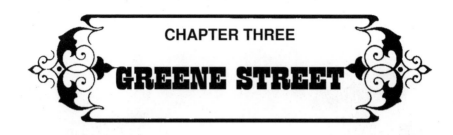

In Silverton's earliest days, before the construction of dance halls and bordellos on Blair Street, prostitution existed. Most of the women worked and lived in the dance halls on the "liquor side of Greene Street." As late as the spring of 1881, the local newspapers were complaining about the fallen women on Greene Street. The _San Juan Herald_ of June 30, 1881, wrote:

> The brazen-faced effrontery shown by some of the Amazons of this town as exhibited upon the public streets and thoroughfares, is becoming a nuisance to every decent and respectable citizen. There are crying evils in every community which it is difficult to surpress, but they should at least be kept within decent boundaries, and if countenanced at all, let it be under the strict surveillance of legal restraint.

ASSAULT AND BATTERY

A serious altercation occurred at the Odeon Dance Hall on Tuesday evening last at 10 o'clock between two frail sirens of that place. The cause was said to be jealousy and resulted in one woman inflicting a severe stab upon the other between the shoulders. The offending party was arrested and given bail, was held for trial till yesterday morning, when a hearing took place before Justice York, and the offender pleaded guilty, was fined the sum of $25 and costs, with a caution from the court not to repeat a similar offense.

Fig. 6   1891 photo of Greene Street showing old Odeon and Westminster Dance Halls.
Ruth Gregory Collection.

The Odeon dance hall was on the east side of Greene Street.[7] At this time the hall was owned by a Mr. John Curry and was leased to Tom Cain. John Curry was the owner and editor of Silverton's first newspaper, the *La Plata Miner*, later to become the *Silverton Miner*. He also owned and edited the Red Mountain newspaper. Tom Cain was a tough Irishman who was later appointed to the post of town marshal. On May 23, 1882, Tom Cain sold his fixtures and stock in his dance hall to his brother, Pat Cain, who would later become a law officer in Rico, Colorado. The bill of sale recorded in the San Juan County Court House gives an insight into the furnishings of an early dance hall and saloon. The list reads as follows:

Tom Cain sold to his brother, Pat Cain of Rico, for $2500 the following, all located in Lot 3, Block 29:

1	piano
4	stoves
8	beds and bedding
10	wash basins
10	pitchers
10	small mirrors
120	gallons of whiskey
5	barrels of beer
2	barrels of cider

1	cook stove and utensels
1	lot dishes
1	bar with fixtures and glassware
1	bar mirror
2	chandeliers and lamps for same
2	bar lamps
3,500	cigars
24	chairs
1	street lamp
1	ice box
60	gallons of wine, blackberry brandy and gin
12	bottles of wine

Notice the listing of eight beds and ten wash basins along with ten pitchers and ten small mirrors. This is not the average furnishings of an early day saloon. The usual procedure was for a miner to come in and buy a dance ticket. The music was provided from a piano and violin or a piano and banjo. For the privilege of dancing he was expected to buy the girl and himself a drink. She was usually served very expensive tea and he cheap whiskey. After the miner consumed enough booze and bought enough dance tickets, the girl would often take him to her room, which was usually a very small cubicle near the rear of the dance hall or upstairs, if the building had two stories. Often by this time, the miner would be blind drunk. It was not uncommon for the woman to "roll" him of what money he had.

Shortly after Tom Cain sold his Odeon Dance Hall to his brother, he purchased the southeast corner of 13th and Blair street from a Mr. Robert Roberts for $1000 and opened a new dance hall. [8] This building was a false-front frame structure.

In July of 1882, the tracks of the Denver & Rio Grande Railroad reached Silverton. This resulted in an explosion of growth and mining in both the town of Silverton and the surrounding hills. An influx of men, followed by the usual contingent of gamblers, saloon keepers, and prostitutes filled the valley. Ground was broken for the new Thomson Block on the northeast corner of 12th and Greene streets. This building was completed in 1883 and was to become the Grand Hotel, now known as the Grand Imperial Hotel. This magnificent building was the showplace of Silverton and much of the west. By 1882, Silverton was boasting a population of, "not far from 3000 inhabitants."

Another addition to the city was the new county jail. This structure was built just off the alley north of the northeast corner of 13th and Blair streets. The building still stands. The August 10, 1882, *San Juan Herald* wrote this about the new jail:

> The exterior of the new stone jail on Blair Street in this city was completed last week, and the interior will soon be in a condition to receive summer boarders, either transiently or permanently, and we venture the assertion that the building is put up in a manner making it impossible for any of the tenants to saw their way out.

The November 9, 1882, *San Juan Herald* wrote of the completed jail:

Fig. 7   Old 1882 stone county jail located in alley between Blair and Mineral streets, just north of 13th Street. 1986. Allan Bird Photo.

OUR NEW COUNTY JAIL

Our county jail has been completed and is ready for use. It is built of granite, and is seventeen-and-one-half by twenty-six feet. The workmanship is of the best character and the materials used are the best that could be procured for the purpose.

The interior arrangement consists of two cells or cages placed in the center of the building. They are made of the best Bristol steel. The cells with corridor to water closet, which is inside the enclosure, are eleven-and-one-half by twenty feet and seven feet in height. The building is heated by a stove placed near the door in the front of building. The water is procured from a cistern located close to the building. A pump has been placed in the Jail within reach of the prisoners. This, with the light, which is admitted through three windows, makes it one of the most comfortable prisons in the State.

The cells are guarded by four locks each and four on the door that leads from the main corridor to the small one inside the enclosure. The outside door is built of solid iron and is guarded by an immense 300-pound lock of the most approved patterns, which, with the cells, were put in place by Mr. M. J. Dorsey. The Jail was built by the Aetna Iron Works.

Over the years the papers listed numerous escapes from this "escape-proof" jail.

The same issue of the paper mentioned the first attempted suicide of a "fallen woman" The article read:

Mollie Durant, the fallen woman who was claimed to have died from an overdose of morphine, did not die from the effect of it. Through medical aid she recovered from the effects of the morphine, but on Tuesday was taken with congestion of the lungs and died in a few hours. Funeral services were held at the house and grave of the poor woman.

By late 1882, the good citizens of Silverton were clamoring for an end to prostitution and dance halls on Greene Street. More and more, the lower element migrated towards Blair. New buildings were being erected every month. Several small cribs were built on the northeast corner lots at 12th and Blair streets, across the street from Jane Bowen's.[9] These cribs were usually rented or owned by women who operated independently, as opposed to women hired to work in a bordello. Holmes and Tewksbury, owners of the corner lot, built a crib and leased it to prostitutes. Next door to the north, Francis Rawley purchased the lot and built her own crib. These cribs were small, one or two room structures.

Robert Roberts owned several pieces of land on Blair and Greene streets. He built saloons and dance halls on his lots. He usually operated one building himself and sold or leased the others. He sold the Blair Street lot south of Tom Cain's to Riley Lambert on November 22, 1882.[10] Lambert proceeded to build a false-front frame dance hall next door to Cain's Dance Hall.

Fig. 8   1884 photo, looking east toward the river, showing Tom Cain's and Riley Lambert's Dance Halls.   Denver Pub. Lib. West. Hist. Dept. Photo.

Fig. 9   Present site of Tom Cain's Dance Hall. Zhivago's Restaurant at right. 1986. Allan Bird Photo.

GREENE STREET

Finally on July 28, 1884, the Town Board decided that there shall be no dance halls "West of the alley lying between Blair and Greene streets." The fine for violation of the ordinance was to be three hundred dollars.

---

[7]   Three doors south of the southeast corner of 12th and Greene.

[8]   This lot would be next door, to the north, of the present-day Zhivago's Restaurant.

[9]   The present Arcade Gift Shop now occupies this corner lot.

[10]   The lot presently occupied by Zhivago's's Restaurant.

CHAPTER FOUR
THE YEAR 1883

The year 1883 was a banner year for the growth of Silverton. The *San Juan Herald* boasted a population in the county of 3500 and almost 2000 for Silverton. Business houses included hotels, five laundries, and twenty-nine saloons. The town treasury was replenished by $5400 from liquor licenses; however, there were only three more licenses issued than in 1882. The March 22, 1883, issue of the *Herald* mentioned that "between fifteen and twenty new buildings have been started in Silverton within the past two weeks. Twelve new buildings have gone up and been completed since January first."

The committee on public buildings recommended that a new city jail be constructed from plank lumber. The April 26, 1883, *San Juan Herald* reported the following:

> The committee on public building recommended the erection of a plank jail, and exhibited drawings. Instructed to prepare for a jail 10 X 25 feet to be made of 2 X 6 plank.

Fig. 10 1883 wooden-plank city jail. Was originally located near the rear of the lot south of the City Hall. Now moved to west side of Greene Street south of 14th Street. (Sign on building says 1893. This is an error) Allan Bird Photo.

24

THE YEAR 1883

May 12, 1883, *San Juan Herald*:

Ross & McKee have the contract for building the city jail, to be built according to the plans and specifications furnished. The price to be paid is $2420, and is to be completed within forty-five days after signing the contract.

June 30, 1883, *Silverton Democrat*:

The calaboose, recently finished in Silverton is indeed a credit to the city, and was constructed under contract by Jim McKay. The entire cost is covered by $2650 and is today a better and more secure building than the county jail. The walls and floors are constructed of 2 X 8 inch planks, thoroughly spiked and solidly built.

This jail was originally located behind the Blair Street City Hall. In recent years it was moved to the west side of Greene Street, and now stands adjacent to the large red sandstone Wyman Building south of 14th Street.

By May 20, the *Silverton Democrat* counted 29 saloons in town, including the row of licensed "houses". The June 16, 1883, *Silverton Democrat* printed an article entitled, "Indictment Against Gambling." It read:

Considerable interest has been taken in the action of the Grand Jury, which brought in 117 indictments against lewd women. When submitted to the court, each and every individual engaged in gambling, was fined $30 and costs, which in all amounts to about $65. Most of them walked to the court and paid their fines without the cause of action, while others awaited the cause of action. Judge Gerry, in performing his duty, gave each offense the least limit of the law, for which he is kindly remembered. Wednesday all gave bond and were released. Upon each and every prostitute, a fine of five dollars and costs were imposed. Dance Halls were fined $25 and costs for keeping open on Sundays and the report that they were to be closed by law is false. They will be allowed to run on Sundays the same as other days.

This would indicate that as of June 16, 1883, there were at least 117 prostitutes working in Silverton. The number would indicate that they were probably working and living on both Blair and Greene streets as late as 1883. It is doubtful that the buildings then in existence on Blair Street would hold 117 women. The above article also illustrates the fact that the laws of Silverton against gambling and prostitution were not made to prevent the two vices but were, in fact, made as a source of revenue for the town coffers. The August 4, 1883, *Silverton Democrat* wrote:

> No effort has yet been made to enforce the new ordinances. The general opinion is, that the council has made an ass of itself and has found it out.

The September 15, 1883, *Silverton Democrat* printed the following comment on the inconsistency of the town laws:

> We have but little use for authorities who prohibit a horse race on Sunday and permit gambling houses and dance halls to run at full blast on that day.

Among the many vices prevalent in Silverton during the early 1880's was one brought by the Chinese; opium joints. The Chinese were considered to be sub-human heathens by the local newspapers. The *Silverton Democrat* of August 4, 1883, printed the following comment:

Judge Earl's office was the scene of a large celestial gathering Wednesday morning. The occasion was the trial of five Chinamen on the charge of smoking opium and it brought together all the pigtails in town. Three were convicted and two more were discharged. Each of the three was fined fifteen dollars and costs, making a grand total of $84.75.

Nineteenth century etching depicting opium den.

The August 25, 1883, *Silverton Democrat* continued:

> It occurs to us that if our city marshal were really desirous of surpressing opium dens in Silverton he would 'pull' a lot of white trash in his raids. It is well known that the Chinamen are not the only ones who frequent these places.

Silverton definitely had a strange set of standards. Gambling and prostitutes were accepted as long as they did not migrate into the "society" section of town, the area known as Quality Hill to the west of Greene Street. The agitation was strong among the churches and the "society people" to outlaw dance halls and prostitution from Greene Street, and confine it to a three block area on Blair Street. When one of the saloon people of either Blair or Greene Streets would move into the "nice" part of town, the _Silverton Democrat_ was quick to respond. The following article was written about Mrs. Ed Gorman. She was probably a girl from the "line." She often provided entertainment in Ed Gorman's Saloon as a singer. When she imbibed the demon rum her character transformed into a "howly terror." The December 13, 1884, issue of the _Silverton Democrat_ reported:

SOMETHING MUST BE DONE

One of the leading citizens, a resident of Snowden Avenue, informs us that Mrs. Ed Gorman, who recently moved into that highly respectable neighborhood of Snowden and Fourteenth street, was making herself a general nuisance again yesterday afternoon, indulging in her usual boisterous and indecent language, greatly to the annoyance and disgust of the ladies living in that immediate vicinity. Such occurrences will soon drive every family from that locality. In fact, today Mr. Fleming is moving his family. This is a grave state of affairs and it lies with the city council to remedy it speedily. James Dyson, the man who rented the house to Mr. Gorman, is the one deserving of attention. He cannot be censured too strongly for renting a building in that part of town to such people. Mr. Gorman himself is a quiet, law-abiding citizen, so far as we know, but all who know his 'wife' represent her as a 'howly terror' when she gets intoxicated and makes life a burden to everybody for blocks around.

During the winter months, things became relatively quiet in Silverton. Many of the women would leave and many of the saloons and hotels would close. The few gambling dens that did remain open continued to do a good business. The November 17, 1883, _Silverton Democrat_ asked the question: "Where does the money come from that is gambled away every day in Silverton? It will take hundreds of dollars to cover it."

CHAPTER FOUR

By the end of 1883, several new bordellos and other buildings had sprung up along Blair Street. The largest of these was built by John Curry, the newspaper man. This building is the second oldest building on Blair Street to have survived until the present. Originally it was known as the Nell Castell House and later became known as the Matties Boarding House. Today it is occupied by an antique shop directly south of Natalia's 1912 Restaurant.[11] The portion of the present building with the ornate iron front, now occupied by the restaurant, was added in 1909. On the same block to the south, two lots north of Alice Morris' early bordello, a small frame house was built by F. O. Sherwood. He leased the building to women of the "line." The corner lot[12] was the former site of a small house built by Theodore Dick for rental to prostitutes. Many of the landlords of the early bordellos were "respectable" Silverton businessmen and women.

Fig. 11 Late 1883 photo blowup of Blair Street between 11th and 12th streets, looking west, showing prominent establishments. Colo. Hist. Soc. Photo.

"BAT" MASTERSON

By the middle of winter, men's tempers would often grow short and trouble would result. Gunplay was relatively infrequent in Silverton; however, when it did occur the results were usually

THE YEAR 1883

serious or fatal. One of the popular myths often repeated in Silverton is the story that the town fathers hired Bat Masterson, of Dodge City fame, to clean up Blair Street. (Actually, they didn't want to clean up their main source of revenue.) Bat Masterson and Doc Holliday did visit Wyatt Earp in the Spring of 1883 when Wyatt was running the gambling rooms of the Arlington Saloon.[13]

Fig. 12 1883 photo of west side of Greene Street, between 13th and 14th streets, showing Arlington Saloon where Wyatt Earp operated the gambling rooms in the spring of 1883. Colo. Hist. Soc. Photo.

The author could find no record that Bat ever worked in Silverton.

The following chapter tells the story of one of Silverton's notorious badmen.

---

[11]   Located two lots south of 12th Street on the west side of Blair Street.

[12]   The lot directly north of Natalia's 1912 Restaurant, now occupied by a modern false-front frame building containing an extension of the Restaurant.

[13]   The Arlington Saloon was located on the west side of Greene Street four doors north of 13th Street.

29

CHAPTER FIVE
TOM CAIN

Tom Cain, the dance hall operator, was elected to the position of town marshal in late August or early September of 1883. Cain was given the responsibility for law and order in Silverton. On November 25, 1883, a shooting occurred between Marshal Cain and his neighbor and competitor, Riley Lambert. The *Silverton Democrat* gave a detailed account of the shooting in the December 1, 1883, issue. The story read as follows:

RILEY LAMBERT SHOT

On Sunday morning last an affray occurred between Riley Lambert, proprietor of one of the dance halls here and Thomas Cain, city marshal, the result of which was to leave both parties wounded. Cain receiving a shot through the right cheek, which was a close call for the jugular vein, and Lambert being shot through the body. The ball entering just below the left nipple, passing diagonally across and under the right set of ribs, being extracted about five inches below the back of the right nipple. Drs. Lawrence and Murray have been in constant attendance on Lambert, but give no encouragement for his recovery as the course of the ball renders it almost a certainty, that the liver was wounded. The facts in regard to this affray as we gathered them from an eyewitness, are as follows: A number of parties who had been up all night in the dance hall, were in the morning making more of a disturbance than the night police deemed proper, and Harry LeRoy went to the hall for the purpose of quieting it. A good deal of loud and threatening talk was being made and LeRoy, thinking that trouble was brewing, left the hall and went to awaken Cain, who was at that time asleep. After doing this he came on the street and saw a man from the dance hall named Leddy going into Posey, Wingate & Heffron's hardware store. Suspecting his errand he promptly followed him and found him buying cartridges. LeRoy arrested him and placed him in the calaboose. Just after doing this Lambert came to the officer and endeavored to secure Leddy's release, which LeRoy could not grant, and while talking with Lambert, Marshal Cain came through the alleyway leading to the jail, and Lambert asked him to release Leddy. This Cain refused to do, saying that in the condition Leddy was in he might make trouble, but agreed to leave the question of his release to the mayor. This plan did not suit Lambert, and exclaiming 'If money won't get him out, this will,' he pulled his pistol and shot Cain, the ball striking him in the face. Cain immediately closed with Lambert and seizing the pistol with his left hand, endeavored to wrest it from him. In the scuffle Lambert shot again, but without effect save the tearing of a large hole in Cain's coat and setting it on fire. By this time Cain had got his pistol out and shot, the ball striking Lambert as before described. Lambert then broke from Cain who fired a second shot, but without effect. Lambert then dropped his pistol, and staggering a few steps sunk to the ground. LeRoy came to him and raising him up, asked him if he was badly hurt, and for reply Lambert took his knife from his pocket and ripped his shirt down, to see the wound himself. By this time other parties appeared on the scene and Lambert was assisted to his room. This account we believe to be substantially correct and fully justifies Marshal Cain by his action. The position he fills is not an enviable one, but he has been a faithful and efficient officer whose whole aim has been to preserve order, and enforce the law. In this he has been, and will be heartily sustained by our citizens, even though he be compelled to resort to the most extreme measures in the performance of his duties.

Later: Lambert died at 4:30 p.m.. on Wednesday.

Riley Lambert left an estate of $10,000 to his brothers. For years after the shooting, the feeling among many of the local people was that Cain shot first. The story reported by the witnesses, who were for the most part Cain's friends, was made up to cover the fact that there had been a long-standing feud between Cain and Lambert. Cain wanted Lambert dead. Shortly before the shooting, Tom's brother, Pat Cain, arrived in Silverton for a visit. By this time Pat had sold his Odeon Dance Hall and was the town marshal of Rico, Colorado. After the shooting, Tom Cain left for six weeks to visit his home in Wisconsin. There was speculation that he would not return.

The next that was heard of Tom Cain was a rather complimentary comment written by the _Silverton Democrat_ on March 22, 1884. It read:

'Law and order' Bosh! Silverton has never been more orderly than it has in the past year. While we are not particularly 'stuck' on Tom Cain, we assert that Silverton has never had a better marshal. That he has not kept order cannot be said by his bitterest enemies.

The following spring Tom and Pat Cain's names came to the forefront again in Silverton. Billy Wilson had been murdered by Pat Cain and Philip Mahar. Tom Cain was deeply involved in the coverup story and bribery of a local judge. On June 22, 1884, the *Silverton Democrat* reported the following story:

> Last Sunday morning (June 22nd) the city was considerably excited over the information that a man had been killed near Silverton. The facts, as near as we can gather, were that Pat Cain, Phil Mahar, and Billy Wilson were out for a ride and started up the road to Red Mountain, and after getting near Burro Bridge, about six miles from town, the three got off to get a drink at a spring, when from some cause firing commenced and Billy Wilson was killed. Cain and Mahar returned to Silverton and surrendered to the authorities. A coroner's jury was impanelled and immediately went to the scene of the affray and after viewing the body it was brought to town and the jury went into secret deliberation. After being in session until Monday evening, they brought in the following verdict: 'We find that the said William Wilson came to his death on the 22d of June, A. D. 1884, about six miles from Silverton on the Ophir and San Miguel toll road, by gunshot wounds from pistols in the hands of Patrick Cain and Phillip Mahar, who did then and there willfully and feloniously kill and murder the said William Wilson within the county of San Juan and state of Colorado.'
>
> The coroner issued a warrant for Cain and Mahar, in accordance with the verdict and they were placed in the county jail. On Tuesday they were arraigned before Justice Bryant and pled not guilty to the charge and were remanded to jail without bail.
>
> It is claimed by the defendants that the shooting of Wilson was in self defense, but as the testimony was not clear on that part they were both held for premeditated murder. The preliminary examination was set for next Monday.
>
> Wilson was a sporting character here and was well known throughout the county. He was 34 years of age and was a native of Wisconsin.
>
> The funeral occurred last Tuesday, and was largely attended. The body was taken to the church where a few appropriate and impressive remarks were made by Rev. Bullock, after which the procession, led by a band playing a dirge, proceeded to the cemetery where the remains were laid to rest.

Evidence surfaced to the effect that Tom Cain had bribed Judge Bryant to release Pat and Phil Mahar on a light bail. The paper came out and openly accused Bryant of taking a bribe even though they could not show definite proof. The paper stirred up the citizens of Silverton and the following letter was the result:

July 3, 1884, *San Juan Herald*:

LETTER TO C. M. BRYANT FROM 'MANY CITIZENS':

Your actions have been very closely watched since the preliminary examination of Cain and Mahar was placed in your hands and while we the citizens, intend that they shall have a trial by jury for the crime they are charged with instead of being lynched, as we don't consider that the man they murdered was any great loss to society, we intend also that the law shall have its course in the premises and as your conduct in the last few days has been somewhat suspicious in conversing with sworn witnesses of Cain and Mahar, and further while we don't wish to intimidate you in any way whatever and while, we have good reason to believe that advances have been made you by Cain's friends we would advise you that it isn't policy for you to be partial towards them in any way whatever. (Signed "Many Citizens")

It is interesting to note that the deciding factor which determined if a man was to by lynched or taken to trial was his worth. When Marshal Ogsbury was killed by Burt Wilkinson in 1879, Wilkinson and the "Copper Colored Kid" were lynched by the mob within a day after their capture because Marshal Ogsbury was "loved by all." Pete Wilson was a saloon bum and pimp. Nobody gave a damn about his fate.

During the following week the case went to trial, and numerous witnesses were called for both the prosecution and the defense. Sheriff William Sullivan testified that Pat and Tom Cain had come into his office to report that Pat and Philip Mahar had shot Billy Wilson in self-defense and wanted to give themselves up. Pat Cain turned over two revolvers to Sullivan, a 38- and a 45-calibre. Pat told Sullivan that Mahar had nothing to do with the shooting. Sheriff Sullivan put both men in the city jail until an investigation of the killing could be made. The sheriff then mounted his horse and rode six miles to the scene of the crime, at Burro Bridge on the road to Red Mountain Town. (the present Ouray road) He reached the body and found a local Silverton man, Tom Moss, sitting on the bank of the stream near the body. Tom handed Sullivan a 41-calibre pistol, that he had found near the body, along with $172.35

plus some jewelry he had found on Wilson's body. Dr. Pascoe and Mike Larnagan were also present when Sullivan arrived.

Tom Moss was called to the stand and placed under oath. He testified that he had met Billy Wilson early that morning and Billy had asked him what he was doing up so early? Tom replied that he was going out to hunt some lost horses. The next time Tom saw Billy, he was lying dead by the roadside near Burro Bridge. Moss said that he had found the 41-calibre pistol lying by Wilson's right hip and a handkerchief by his left hand. There was a large pool of blood in the road about 30 paces from where he had found the body. Tom Moss told the court that his first thought was that Wilson had committed suicide.

Dr. Pascoe testified that he was on his way to Chattanooga, a small community on the road to Red Mountain Town, when he found the body. Wilson was lying on his back and had apparently been moved from where he had died. Dr. Pascoe said that it looked to him that the pistol had been placed by his side.

Pat Cain was next called to the stand. Pat claimed that he and Philip Mahar were planning a trip to Ophir and invited Billy to join them. He agreed and the three stopped off at Goode's Saloon for a drink and some cigars. Before leaving town, they stopped at the new beer garden, which was located near the Martha Rose Smelter, for another drink. When they reached Burro Bridge, they dismounted to get a drink of water from a spring. Wilson said he saw a rabbit and asked Phil for his gun. Phil handed him his 41-revolver and he immediately leveled the gun at Pat saying, "Cain, defend yourself," at the same time firing a shot. Billy missed and Cain drew both of his revolvers, a 41- and 45-, and started firing. According to Cain, Wilson got off three shots before he was hit by Cain's fire. Cain swore that all three men were sober, even though they had stopped for a few drinks before leaving town.

Philip Mahar was called next. He concurred with Pat Cain's testimony but said he had obtained his gun, a 41-calibre revolver, from Ed Gorman's bar early that morning. In later testimony, both Ed Welch, Gorman's bartender, and Ed Gorman denied that they had given Mahar a gun.

Wilson's girl friend, Nellie vanCamp, was called to the stand. She stated that she had been living with Billy for three years. She further testified that Billy had left his gun in the room that morning. Nellie was one of the Blair Street "working girls." Billy was her pimp.

The next witness was a J. W. Heck. He told the court that he was coming from Ophir to Silverton that morning, and had made an examination of the ground where Wilson was shot. He had found a pool of blood a short distance from where Wilson's body lay. In the blood-soaked ground he had found a flattened bullet containing matted hair. He produced the bullet and made a diagram for the court. The court ordered that the bullet be weighed. It weighed 190 grains, about the weight of a 38-calibre slug.

Joe Allen, the operator of the beer garden near the Martha Rose Smelter at the edge of town, testified that the three men had stopped at his place for a beer. While Wilson and Mahar were drinking their beer, Cain went outside and discharged both of his guns. Wilson reached in his pocket and discovered that he had left his gun at home. He asked Allen if he could borrow a gun. Allen told him he didn't have a gun.

The post-mortem examination was made by Drs. Lawrence, Brown, Presby, and Pascoe. They testified that Wilson had been shot six times, with two balls entering the right side, one the left side, two entering the left side of the head (leaving severe powder burns), and one in the left forearm. Dr. Lawrence produced a bullet he had taken from Wilson's head. It weighed 195 grains.

Two witnesses who lived near Burro Bridge were called. D. J. Well, said that he had heard four shots, the last two were fired together. L. S. Robertson, who also lives in a cabin near Burro Bridge said that he had heard at least three shots, possibly more.

The next witness presented a damaging case against the defense. Mr. C. F. McCoin stated that he did not know Wilson but he did know Cain. He said that he had found three riderless horses heading for Silverton. He caught the horses and shortly after encountered Cain and Mahar on foot. He claimed that Cain remarked "we got our man, all the same." Mahar countered with "What's that?" Cain bragged, "Well at least I did."

The defense called Tom Cain to the stand. Tom's story was that he was in bed when his brother Pat and Phil Mahar came into his room. Pat told him that he had run into some trouble up the road and needed some 41- and 45-calibre cartridges. Tom said that he did not have any 41's but that he had a box of 45's he was welcome to use. He also told Pat to leave his 41-gun and take Tom's 38-calibre pistol, which was loaded. After Pat and Phil told Tom what had happened, Tom suggested that they go to Billy Sullivan and give themselves up, which they did.

Several of Tom Cain's friends were trying to help with the coverup, but many ended up contradicting each other. Tom testified that he had given Pat the 38-. H. A. Van Lugar, Tom's bartender testified that he was the one that had given Pat the 38. Butch Waggoner claimed he was present when Van Lugar exchanged Pat's 41 for the 38. Waggoner was a gambler working in Tom Cain's Blair Street dance hall. Several of Tom Cain's friends testified that they had heard Billy Wilson make brags that "If he could get a show, he would kill both of those d-n s-ns of b-s." A gambler, James Collins, testified that when he was attending the February term of court at Gunnison, that Wilson told him, "Tom Cain had killed his best friend, Riley Lambert, and that he had taken a shot at Tom but had missed." A dance hall rustler, William Leonard, testified that Wilson had told him "that he had just been waiting for the snow to go off so he could do up those Cains."

D. L. Mechling had weighed two 41-calibre slugs for the court. He reported that one weighed 203 grains and the other 205 grains.

Finally, Sheriff Sullivan was called back to the stand. He told the court that Pat Cain had said nothing to him about exchanging guns. He said Cain gave Sullivan a 38 and a 45.

Most of the witnesses for the defense were part of Tom Cain's "gang." They were all bar owners, bartenders, gamblers or pimps. If what they said about Billy Wilson's threats to kill the Cains was true, it is highly unlikely that Wilson would be taking an early morning ride with the Cain clan without his gun. Perhaps the most convincing testimony against Cain and Mahar was the report by the two men who lived near the scene of the crime. One had heard three shots, "possibly more." The other had heard four with the last two shots being fired together. Since there were six bullet holes in Wilson, this would indicate that Cain had fired both of his guns simultaneously twice so as to sound like two shots instead of four. The last two shots "fired close together" were the final execution shots to Wilson's head while he was lying on the ground dying.

The exchange of guns story cooked up by Tom Cain was to explain what happened to Pat Cain's 41-calibre pistol. Wilson was supposed to have borrowed Mahar's 41-pistol. Since they left a 41 next to the body, they were short a pistol. Actually, Mahar was carrying a 38-calibre pistol. After Pat Cain murdered Billy Wilson, Phil Mahar finished him off with his 38. They left Pat's 41 behind to back their very weak story. The two bullets that entered Wilson's head were 38's. They were not smart enough to leave the body where it fell. It is doubtful that a man with six bullet holes in him, including two through the head, is going to get up and move 30 paces carrying his gun with him. This was probably the most cold-blooded murder in the history of Silverton. The coroner's jury came to the same conclusion.

The people of Silverton were furious when Judge Bryant released Cain and Mahar on a light bail. Pat Cain's bond was set at $2000 and Mahar's at $200. The bondsmen were Tom Cain, Joe Stender, a saloon owner, and John Murphy. The paper reported that "groups of men could be seen on every corner all day Monday discussing the matter. Sentiment of the community could not be misunderstood." One citizen reported that he knew for a fact that Judge Bryant had spent the night meeting secretly with Tom Cain. To further back the accusation that Bryant had been bribed, Pat Cain's friends from Rico went home on Saturday and remarked to

parties that they met on the road "that everything was all right."
Judge Bryant left town on Monday, "beastly drunk," for the
Sheridan Mine in Marshall Basin where he was employed as an ore
sorter. This tells something about the quality of early day law in
Silverton. The July 12, 1884, *Silverton Democrat* printed the
following article about Bryant:

> The best thing we have heard on Bryant was by Lawyer Gray.
> Monday evening Bryant rode up to his office on a mule and dismounted.
> While hitching the animal it kept up a continuous braying, much to the
> annoyance of Bryant. Mr. Gray, who was standing nearby, noticed
> Bryant's discomfiture and called out to him, 'That's the ghost of the
> murdered Wilson.' Bryant made no reply, but sneaked into his office.

Shortly after Cain and Mahar were released on bail, the
Telluride Evening News printed the following story about their
movements:

> Pat Cain and Phil Mahar were seen one day last week near the state
> line going in the direction of Utah. Both were mounted on fine horses and
> they were armed to the teeth. They also had a pack animal along which
> carried their blankets, etc. It is supposed they were taking a French
> leave.

The editor of the *Silverton Democrat*, Mr. H. M. Condict, wrote
the story of the Wilson murder as he, and most everyone in town,
saw it, based on the testimony of the above witnesses. Tom Cain,
in a fit of temper, vowed "to 'fix' Condict if he ever mentioned Tom's
or Pat Cain's name in his d—n paper again." Condict continued to
print the story at the risk of his life.

On the night of August 8, 1884, Editor Condict was having a
drink with Dick Journey, mine superintendent of the National
Belle Mine, at M. K. Cohen's Arion Hall.[14] Tom Cain entered with
a gang of his henchmen. One of the gang, a man by the name of
"Dutchy", picked a fight with Jacob Schaefor and was "abusing him
shamefully." Condict remarked to Journey that he would like to
see "Dutchy" get licked. Tom Cain overheard the remark, and
immediately his gang surrounded Condict and Journey at their
table. Cain collared Condict with the remark, "By God, maybe you

would like to do it." Cain held Condict by the collar, and began abusing him for the stories he had printed about the Cain-Mahar murder trial. In the course of the threats, Cain told Condict, "If you ever mention Tom Cain's name or my brothers in your G-d d—n paper again there will be one Jim Crow editor that'll not write anything more." Condict and Journey were at a great disadvantage being pinned in their chairs, they could do nothing. Shortly after, Cain and his gang left and Condict and Journey started home. They were crossing the street between the bank and Stender and Ryan's place[15] when Cain called to them to stop. They stopped. Cain and his gang started to rough them up again when the town policeman arrived on the scene. Cain told Policeman Kilbourne that if he had not been present it would have been much worse for Condict.

Condict immediately printed the story of Cain's threats in his paper. He stated that "Tom Cain has promised to 'fix' us if his or his brother's name is ever again mentioned in the Democrat. It is

Fig. 13 View of east side of Greene Street between 12th and 14th streets. Notice M. K. Cohen's Arion Hall where Tom Cain threatened to "Fix" Editor Condict. Photo taken about 1886. Denver Pub. Lib. West. Hist Dept.

consoling to know that we will not be the first he has ever 'fixed'."
He also called on the good people of Silverton to drive men like Cain
out of town. He reminded his readers that:

> This same Tom Cain has passed as a 'badman' ever since he has
> been in the country; he is the man who fired into a crowd at Silver Cliff
> in 1878 and killed an innocent man for which he has never been tried;
> he is the man who killed Riley Lambert; he is the man who has made
> several uncalled for gun plays in Silverton; he is the man upon whom
> suspicion rests heavily on account of the murder of Wilson; he is the man
> who runs a dance hall and keeps a woman, and he is the infamous cur
> that seeks to stifle public opinion by threats of violence and intimida-
> tions.

Editor Condict was an extremely courageous man. Even the
Denver Press printed articles commending his brave actions.

Shortly after the above threats by Cain, Condict filed a formal
complaint against Cain for threatening his life. The case went to
trial and Cain was found guilty. Justice Earl heard the case and
released Tom Cain on a $300 bond. The other witnesses were to put
up a $150 bond to assure that they would show up for the district
court trial. Condict was elated that the courts finally found Cain
guilty of something. He didn't think that the $300 bail would deter
Cain from leaving the country but at least he hoped it would teach
Cain that he could not muzzle the press. He wrote in his August 16
issue, "We shall write up Mr. Cain, or Mr. Smith, or Mr. Brown, or
Mr. Jones whenever we feel so disposed and shall say exactly what
our judgment dictates is right, without fear or favor."

H. M. Condict won a moral victory over Tom Cain, however,
the bond set by Judge Earl was never put up. In a comedy scene of
early Silverton law, Judge Earl was called up by the district court
to explain why the bond was not paid. The following direct testimony of the court reveals the lax nature of 1884 law:

The following is a summary of the court's censure of Justice W.
E. Earl printed in the September 6, 1884, *Silverton Democrat*:

TOM CAIN

Justice W. E. Earl

'Mr. Earl, please take the stand.'

'Mr. Earl, do you remember of having heard a case on or about August 11, 1884, wherein the people of the State of Colorado were plaintiffs and Thomas Cain defendant?'

'Yes sir'

'Can you now call to mind the result of that trial?'

'Yes, I held the defendant under $300 bond and the state witnesses under $150 each.'

'Now, Mr. Earl, will you please state to the court (the people) whether the bonds of the state witnesses were ever required or not?'

'They were not'

'Yes. Well, now did or did not Mr. Condict, the prosecuting witness, call upon you on more than one occasion for the purpose of furnishing his required bond?'

'He did'

'Was the bond of the defendant Cain, ever required?'

'It was not'

'Did you deliver to the District Court the proceedings in the case as you are required by law to do?'

'I did not'

'And can you give any satisfactory explanation of your actions in this matter—the palpable neglect of many of your duties as a justice of the peace?'

Just here a dog fight occurred in front of the Democrat office and the witness was so much interested that he adjourned himself and we have been unable to get him on the stand since.

However, the use of our columns are hereby tendered the gentleman for the purpose of giving his answer to an anxious constituency.

Condict collected items from the _Denver Press_ about his heroic stand against the Cain gang. He was quick to print the comments of the "state" press. "The state press is unanimous in its praise of the Democrat's fearless denunciation of Tom Cain and his layout."

Editor Condict was furious over Judge Bryant's release of Pat Cain and Phil Mahar on such a light bond. As was expected, both Cain and Mahar skipped town and their whereabouts was unknown. Condict wrote the following plea to the governor in the September 6, 1884, _Silverton Democrat_: "The Governor should at once offer a large reward for the apprehension of Pat Cain and Phil Mahar, the murderers of Billy Wilson."

CHAPTER FIVE

Condict continued his assault on Justice Bryant. It is obvious that libel suits were not the "in thing" during the 1880's. He wrote, also on September 6, 1884, the following:

> It is believed that an earnest effort was made by the grand jury to find sufficient evidence to indict the late Justice Cushing M. Bryant for bribery. No doubt of his guilt rests in the mind of any man acquainted with the circumstances, but it is an impossible matter to get positive evidence.

Editor Condict's efforts to obtain justice against Tom Cain were finally rewarded. Cain was not only indicted for threatening Condict's life, but also for a shooting spree which occurred during the summer in the Fashion Saloon.[16]

TOM CAIN INDICTED

> We take great pleasure in informing the few remaining friends of Tom Cain that we have pretty straight information of the gentlemen's indictment by the grand jury this week. A true bill was found against Thomas for his little gun play on Fatty Collins at the Fashion Saloon in the early part of the summer. Thus, 'one by one the roses fall'—when they monkey with the editor.

When Pat Cain and Phillip Mahar jumped bail and left the country, the bondsmen were left owing the county $2200. Tom Cain, along with the other bondsmen suggested that the county take Cain's Dance Hall in lieu of the $2200 bond. The attorneys for the people consulted several real estate people and the concensus was that Tom Cain's Blair Street dance hall was worth $3000. Mr. Stender, one of the bondholders, suggested that the county issue $400 in county script to the three bondholders to offset the difference between the required bond and the higher value of the dance hall. This deal was accepted against complaints of the Democrat that the property was only worth $1500 at best. It would be better to get the $1500 than nothing, which is what they would have received from Cain and the other bondholders in a years time.

To make a long story short, the town of Silverton ended up owning Tom Cain's Saloon and Dance Hall on the southeast corner of 13th and Blair Streets. At one time, they moved the town offices to the old saloon. Thus one of Blair Street's early bordellos became the local office of the Town of Silverton.

TOM CAIN

Tom Cain lost his saloon and dance hall and immediately left Silverton for the Arizona Territory. He moved to Ash Fork and opened another dance hall. It was rumored that his brother Pat was living with him. News of the following nature reached Silverton:

October 4, 1884, *Silverton Democrat*:

> Information was received in Silverton this week that one more unfortunate has met, at the hands of the Cain outfit, that peculiar treatment known as 'fixing.' In other words, about the 20th of last month, at Ash Fork, A. T. (Arizona Territory) it is currently rumored that (Tom and Pat Cain) got into a slight altercation with a miner at that place and deliberately shot him dead. Further particulars we have been unable to learn.

Shortly after the above article was received, Tom Cain met his equal and the old adage that "he who lives by the gun, dies by the gun" came true.

November 29, 1884, *Silverton Democrat*:

TOM CAIN REPORTED KILLED

> Mr. Robert Roberts, of this city, received yesterday morning a telegram from Ash Fork, A. T., and signed by Wm. Leonard, which stated that Tom Cain was killed in that place the night before. We have been unable to obtain further particulars up to the hour of going to press. Tom Cain, it will be remembered, formerly ran a dance hall in this place; shot Riley Lambert November 25th last year, and his skirts were not entirely clear of the Wilson murder. His reputation was very bad throughout southern Colorado, where he was well known.

December 6, 1884, *Silverton Democrat*:

THE CAIN HOMICIDE

> There now seems little doubt that Tom Cain has 'passed in his checks.' There was much doubt in the minds of many as to whether the Leonard telegram was genuine and correct. That telegram arrived about noon Thursday, the 27th, and stated 'Tom Cain was killed at 1 o'clock this morning.' the suspicion that this telegram was bogus was greatly strengthened on Thursday of this week, when Mattie Cook received a letter from her sister who lives in Albuquerque, stating that it is 'Jim' Marshall who was killed at Ash Fork, A. T., on Thanksgiving morning.

CHAPTER FIVE

Later in the same day that Mattie Cook received her letter, William Snyder received a telegram from M. B. ('Jim') Marshall. The telegram was as follows, and was sent in answer to a letter of inquiry addressed to Marshall, immediately after the first news of Cain's murder was received:

'Ash Fork, A. T., December 4, 1884,—Just received your letter, Leonard's dispatch is correct. I was in Prescott at the time. He was shot on the 27th of November. Got 18 buckshot in his breast. Was shot by a teamster by the name of Evans, who got clear.'

'M. B. Marshall'

The article continued:

From the above it would appear that the man Evans was justified in what he did. From all we can gather the circumstances are as follows: Cain and Marshall were running a sort of variety show and dance hall at Ash Fork. It was after the show and during the dance that Cain got into trouble with Evans over eighty cents. Cain began his characteristic bluster, accompanied by his promise to 'do him (Evans) up.' Evans told him he was unarmed and Cain then said: 'Well, go and fix yourself, and that God d—n quick, too, and I'll settle this matter with you.' It appears that the man went out and procured a heavily loaded double-barreled shot gun and returned to the dance hall. Just as he stepped in the door he called to Cain. 'Are you ready?' Cain replied 'yes,' and reached for his gun. As Cain turned fairly facing Evans, the latter discharged both barrels of his gun at once. Eighteen buck-shot taking effect in his breast as stated in the telegram quoted above. Cain fired one shot as he fell, it going through the ceiling. Evans gave himself up and was cleared at the preliminary examination.

So ends the story of Tom Cain, one of Silverton's earliest saloon and dance hall operators.

---

14   The present site of the French Bakery dining room located on the ground floor of the Teller House on Greene Street, just south of 13th Street.

15   The two south corners of 13th and Greene streets.

16   The "Fashion" was a two-story frame building located on the east side of Greene Street, about the middle of the block opposite the Grand Imperial Hotel.

44

CHAPTER SIX

WHY GIRLS GO BAD

What's a nice girl like you doing in a place like this? The question often asked in the early-day bordellos. During the late Victorian and early nineteen hundreds, the social conditions for women were deplorable. Women had few choices with their lives. They could become housewives and mothers, the preferred occupation, or they could work at menial jobs such as dress-makers or servants. It is little wonder that many chose the "easy way" out. The September 19, 1885, *La Plata Miner* reprinted an article published by the *New York Graphic* which read as follows:

NEW YORK SHOP GIRLS

Temptation To Which Many Of Them Are Constantly Exposed

Much has been said and much more has been written for and against the publication of the *Paul Maul Gazette* in regard to the sacrifice of young girls to the unholy passions of men. One has but to keep his eyes open to see how young girls are tempted to enter a life of shame. Just look around the next time you happen to be in one of the large dry goods houses in this city and you will very soon see what class of people get the most attention. If you are a lady, dress yourself quietly and enter one of these establishments without ostentation and then observe the difference between your reception and that of some handsomely dressed but notorious member of the demimonde. Note the obsequious manner of floorwalker and salesman, the admiring glances of those standing near the creature, all intent on the words that fall from her painted lips and almost indifferent to the wants of more modest customers. If you chance to be buying at the same counter you will find it almost impossible to retain the attention of the salesman who is waiting on you sufficiently to enable you to make a selection of goods. It matters not whether you do or do not, all eyes are on the bedizened courtezan and the sooner you leave the counter the better all are pleased. This is not a fancy sketch but is the truth, and what must be thought by the poor girls behind adjoining counters who are working hard to make an honest living when they contrast the manner of these men toward themselves and these brazen creatures? Must the temptation not be great to get away from a life of toil and hardships and will not that temptation grow until, when chance offers, they are but the ready victim to some unscrupulous roue?

I heard a story of a young girl not long since whom I knew to be honest, upright and truthful. She told me of her struggle to gain a position where she could support herself. Among other places she applied to a certain establishment for a position as saleswoman. Being bright and pleasant in her manners, she was taken to the proprietor and he being pleased with her appearance offered her a position and mentioned the salary she might expect. 'Why Mr.___.' she exclaimed, 'that would not support a child much less a grown woman.' The proprietor looked at her a moment and then said 'Of course I know you could not live on that but haven't you a gentleman friend to help you out with your expenses?' The girl was too dumbfounded to speak. The tone and look which accompanied them being more than the words. 'We pay none of our saleswoman more than that,' he added, and the girl took her departure in tears. 'Oh how I hate that man,' she concluded.

Can one wonder then, that in this great city full of temptation, men find ready victims among their 'lawful prey?' And what can be done? Simply nothing. What woman will weigh against the obsequious attentions of men to the painted courtezans at the stores and the sight of a noted actress seated by the side of her no less noted lover on their way to the park for their evening drive, when the poor girls, each of whom is prettier than the objects of their admiration, are coming home tired and worn out with the day's hard work and the constant nagging of the floorwalker? Who can blame them when a silent vow is registered to escape this life of hard work and paltry pay for one that to them looks easy and filled only with pleasure and comfort? They do not see the backward glance the favored actress gives, nor hear the sighs she heaves as her glance falls on some bright young face in the crowd. Nor can they know the heartfelt wish that she was even as one of these and innocent as they. But Mephistopheles is by her side and the sigh is soon followed by a smile. The smile only is noted and envied by the tired girls.

The average wage of a house servant in Silverton was $30 a month. For this they were expected to work long hours, seven days a week. Often the misery of being a household domestic was more than a young girl could bear. The January 24, 1903, *Silverton Standard* documents the dire results of this type of life:

> Friday forenoon about 11:30 o'clock, Delia Curry, a domestic who has been employed in various households in Silverton for the past year, attempted suicide by swallowing carbolic acid. The deed was committed at the Baremouth Hotel, where the girl was temporarily stopping, and it was some time before it was realized what she had done and physicians were called, which makes the case extremely hard to handle. No reason known at this time for the rash act except perhaps despondency. As we go to press this afternoon (Friday), the physicians are working to save the girl's life, but the results are uncertain.
>
> Note: She died at 3 o'clock Saturday morning.

The lure of fancy clothes and the deceptive "easy life" of prostitution often led young girls away from their chosen way of life. The law was very strict about "nice" girls being found in the red light district. The July 29, 1899, *Silverton Standard* tells of one such girl being found in a dance hall:

> Thursday night a waitress in one of our boarding houses just went out for a 'minute or two' and was found by nightwatch Leonard at about midnight in one of the dance halls, drunker than a fiddler. The event was but a repetition of the girl's old tricks. She is young, her parents reside here and if they have no control over her she should be sent to the home for incorrigibles.

Housewives were often prime candidates for prostitution. Often women were married to drunkards or wife beaters and life at home became unbearable. Divorce was almost as shameful as prostitution so the end result was that many of the girls on the "line" were married. A strange case of a man finding his wife in a Blair Street bordello was reported in the November 29, 1902, *Silverton Standard* in which a clairvoyant directed the man to Silverton. The story reads as follows:

> Ed Harless, a Victor business man, arrived in Silverton yesterday in search of a runaway wife and in the afternoon, in company with Marshal Leonard, located her on Blair Street. When the two men entered the room the officer stepped to the window to let in some light and while doing this was startled by the woman's screams and turned in time to

see the husband drawing an ugly looking revolver, but was prevented from using it by the prompt action of Leonard, who wrestled the weapon away from Harless and lodged him in jail. Later Police Judge Hodges fined the Victor man $50 and costs, in default of which he is yet in duranceville.

December 6, 1902, *Silverton Standard*:

Ed Harless had a 'hunch' and after a few days in our city jail and paying a small assessment by the police magistrate, returned to his Denver home to interview a certain clairvoyant that will divulge the secret of the whereabouts of the Telluride assassin. Harless by the same spirit medium was told that his wife was in Silverton, where he came in search of her last week, finding her in the tenderloin district, proceeded to end her life with a 45-Colts but was prevented from so doing by the prompt action of Marshal Leonard.

Many of the women of the "row" or "line" were very generous, good-hearted people. In interviewing people who knew these women, most related stories of charity and sacrifice for others. During the deadly flu epidemic of 1918 many served as nurses. During the depression of the 1930's, often food was delivered by way of the back door to hungry families by women of the "line." Even the paper wrote of their charity, at the same time chastising the "Christians" in town. The January 17, 1891, *Silverton Standard* wrote of a poor young girl with a new baby and two small children that had been abandoned by her husband. The story read as follows:

Sometimes we feel like preaching a little sermon ourselves. The case of Mrs. Gallagher is a good text. Here is a woman with a baby, eight weeks old, and two other children to care for. Her husband neglects her and has failed to provide food since the baby was born. Who came to this woman's assistance? Christianity? No. Charity? Yes. And where did the charity come from? From the Christians, as this world judges? No. But every Jericho has a Rahab, and many a Rahab has done acts of charity, as in this case, which should make some Christians blush. What a narrow minded people we are; too hasty to condemn too slow to forgive. But blood is thicker than water, and that which flows through the veins of those, whom some call lost, may show more Christian charity than all the blue bloods of a would-be-aristocracy—and often time it does.

WHY GIRLS GO BAD

This is not to imply that life on the "line" was sweet and glamorous. From what we can gather from the newspaper reports of the fighting, robbery, and death from both disease and suicide, life on the "line" was a living hell.

The early day mine owners considered the bordellos a social necessity for the well-being of their miners. The ratio of men to women in early day Silverton was about eighteen to one. Another problem existed with the few marriageable women. The August 23, 1884, _Silverton Standard_ summarized the situation:

WHY GIRLS DON'T MARRY OUT WEST

There is mighty little marrying and giving in marriage here. The men don't seem to be anxious about it, and the girls are so well up to snuff that they won't encourage a man till they know his former life and make sure he has not a surplus wife or two somewhere in the east.

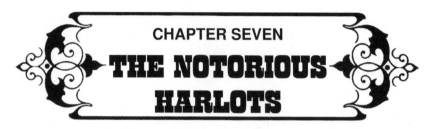

CHAPTER SEVEN
THE NOTORIOUS HARLOTS

Of the hundreds of women who worked as prostitutes in early-day Silverton, a few gained special recognition through their violent actions. The local newspapers usually did not dwell on the red light district except when events got out of hand and somebody was robbed or hurt. It then depended upon who was robbed or hurt. The August 23, 1884, _Silverton Democrat_ printed the following story:

> A Mexican had one of the Blair Street angels arrested for stealing some money the other night. That Mexican was evidently not acquainted with the usages of good society in Silverton. He not only did not recover his money, but had to pay the costs of the trial.

MOLLY FOLEY

A large proportion of the women who worked on the "line" were rather violent by nature. The Police Court weekly reported the names of several of the more unruly ones and fined them the usual $14.75. Fighting among the girls and also among the girls and their customers was a weekly occurrence. Certain women made the news on a more-or-less regular basis and these soon became branded as "notorious." Perhaps the most famous of these was Molly Foley. She was one of the oldest in both age and arrival in Silverton. Molly was born in Scotland in December 1836. She arrived in Colorado in 1864 at the age of 28, working as a prostitute in the frontier camps of Chama, New Mexico, Animas City and Durango, Colorado, and many of the early mining and railroad camps. Molly was a tall, attractive girl and was a favorite of the early-day Silverton miners. She arrived in Silverton in 1878 at the age of forty-two. Because of her age, she became a Madame and ran a small independent crib with a few girls working for her.

THE NOTORIOUS HARLOTS

The first mention of Molly in the Silverton paper was on September 3, 1887, when the *Silverton Democrat* printed the following story:

> Several of the keepers of Blair Street resorts have recently been disregarding the ordinances of the town of Silverton by selling beer without procuring a town license. Molly Foley was arrested Thursday upon a charge of this character and was tried yesterday before Justice B. O'Driscoll. The evidence was not sufficient to warrant conviction; the prisoner was discharged. J. W. Cory was the attorney for the defense.

The following year, on November 10, 1888, Molly again made the news with a spectacular fist fight with another of the more notorious women of the "line," Lizzie Fisher. The *San Juan Democrat* did a magnificent job of describing the fight, round by round:

> Two fair but frail maidens of Blair Street fame sailing under the euphonious titles of Molly Foley and Lizzie Fisher, had a slight altercation last Saturday, and they proceeded to demolish each other with Spartan-like heroism. Molly led off with a vicious right hander and smote Lizzie in the left optic, almost obscuring her vision. This caused Lizzie's blood to rise ten degrees in the thermometer and she led off with a vicious left-hander on Molly's larder almost knocking the breath of life out of her. Hostilities then ceased for a time, and when they had gotten their breaths, again they proceeded with Sullivan-like viciousness to the combat. Lizzie being shorter and more vicious than her tall antagonist, led off with a wicked left-hander and caromed on Molly's lower ribs, brasing them to the Queen's taste, causing her bustle to stick out too much and bringing tears to her eyes. After recovering from this blow, and now being stung to fury, Molly led out with a paralyzing blow and erected a good sized shanty on the vacant lot between Lizzie's right eye and nose, and painting it a dark blue. At this point the referee declared a draw as Joe Martin and Marshal Snowden were hovering around, and the procession halted. The trouble arose over one of them wounding the young and tender affections of the other. (Molly was fifty-one years old at the time.)

Lizzie Fisher's career somewhat paralleled Molly Foley's. She arrived in Silverton in the spring of 1884 and was arrested on October 14, 1884, for being a 'lady of easy virtue.' She died of peritonitis on October 2, 1904. Her real name was Lizzie Thompson. Her funeral was held in the undertaking rooms of L. G. Prosser and she was buried in the Hillside Cemetery at Silverton.

CHAPTER SEVEN

A year later the _Silverton Standard_ printed another short article about Molly's violent life:

> Molly Foley swore out a warrant four months ago against Bill Kingman for assault. Bill had been away and only returned two days since, when the nightwatch gathered him in. Mrs. Foley withdrew the suit and paid the costs.

Again on January 17, 1891, the _Standard_ printed the report of yet another fight:

> Madame Molly Foley contributed $50 to the city this week for trying to reduce a companion's expenses this winter by fixing her head so that she could eat hay.

The people of Silverton didn't know how tough Molly really was. The _Standard_ , on November 26, 1896, printed her obituary which read:

> One of Blair Streets unfortunates, Molly Foley, died last Thursday.

Quoting Mark Twain, "The reports of her death were greatly exaggerated." Molly refused to die and her name cropped up again on April 15, 1899. She was now sixty-two years old. The _Silverton Standard_ read:

> Yesterday afternoon between the hours of three and four, while under the influence of liquor in the den of Molly Foley, William Davenport stabbed Sam Hall, cutting a deep and ugly wound between the shoulder blades. Davenport was lodged in the county jail where he awaits preliminary examination and when a more and full explanation will be given in the cause of his actions. The wound in Hall's back is of such a nature that it will require some days to ascertain whether serious or not.

Note: The following week the paper reported that Hall was on the road to recovery.

At a later trial, charges were dropped against Davenport as he claimed self defense and the court upheld his claim.

The July 14, 1899, *Silverton Standard* printed the following story about one of Molly's girls:

ONE MORE UNFORTUNATE

A woman, one of Blair Street's unfortunates, known as May Rikard, died in the cabin of Molly Foley at an early hour Tuesday morning. The poor outcast without friends or home, after a night of carousing at one of the dance halls, laid down on her bed and sank into her last sleep. Very likely the world has been but a channel house of blasted hopes to her for years and, without doubt, the transition from a living death to the grave, were a relief. All of these fallen women have heart histories, dating backward from childhood's happy hour to the bleak existence cast upon them later on. Repentance is an easy word and conveys a lot of meaning. In the case of the fallen women, however, there's generally an insurmountable barrier to its attainment. Not often does the cloak of charity fall from a sneering, pelting world upon a Magdalen.

The body was examined by Coroner Prosser and County Physician Prewitt, no marks of violence were found upon it. Mr. Prosser's opinion was that the women died from alcoholism. The deceased, it is stated by those living with her, said she had taken a dose of morphine about midnight. No inquest was held and the remains were buried by acquaintances who solicited subscriptions for that purpose.

This obituary sums up the total despair and poverty that many of these girls faced and society's attitude toward them. Almost, without exception, the girls who died from disease or suicide did not have enough money to pay for their simple funerals.

We do not know the location of Molly Foley's crib. In 1901, she did occupy one room of a three-crib building next door to the National Hall.[17]   During her last years she shared a small cabin with "Denver" Kate, behind the second French Bakery, built on the site of Tom Cain's Dance Hall. Both Molly and Kate spent their last years doing laundry and cleaning for the younger girls of Blair Street. Molly died in 1914 at the age of seventy-eight. "Denver" Kate put two daughters through the University of Colorado. They never knew what their mother did for a living. Kate moved to a small cabin on the southwest corner of Blair and 12th streets. She died in 1925.

The story was related to the author by a man who was a teenager in 1910. He told of how the old men could go to Molly's cabin and get "it" for fifty cents when the going rate on the "line" was $2.

Molly's obituary was printed in the January 2, 1915, _Silverton Standard_ and read as follows:

> The death of Molly Foley, which occurred last Tuesday evening, (December 28, 1914) marked the passing of one of the most notorious characters known to the San Juan district. She came here thirty-six years ago (1878) after an eventful career in Chama, Animas City, Durango, and many of the early frontier camps. She was formerly noted for her vivacity, neatness of dress and generosity. To those who knew her in late years, crippled and dejected, it would be hard to recognize any of the charms that made her attractive in the days of the prairie schooners. She was about seventy-eight years of age, and left no known relatives. The funeral was held Thursday from McCleod's undertaking parlors.

Molly was buried on New Years Eve in Hillside Cemetery, Silverton, Colorado.

BLANCHE DEVILLE

Blanche DeVille was another of the early Silverton prostitutes. The first news of Blanche was in the _Silverton Democrat_ of September 6, 1884, when she was indicted for larceny. Her weakness appeared to be stealing. On September 13, 1884, she was again arrested for rolling John Fernando. Three days later she was arrested for stealing $12 from one of her fellow prostitutes, Annie Williams. Two days later she was indicted by the grand jury for stealing $50 from another soiled dove, Jessie Carroll. She was forced to put up $200 bond. The September 18, 1884, _San Juan Herald_ documented the case:

> Blanche DeVille was indicted by the grand jury in stealing $50 from Jessie Carroll. She had been bound over in the sum of $200 by Justice Earl for the same offense and she left town. Deputy Sheriff LeRoy went to Durango but could not find her. Her bondsman, not willing to lose $200, went after her and brought her back, and retained John G. Taylor

to defend her. The case was set down for trial in the morning of the twelfth, when District Attorney Rood stated to Judge Gerry that he would nolle (cancel) the case of grand larceny, and the defendant would plead guilty to the other indictment of assault and battery upon Jessie Carroll. That he had examined the matter, and thought that a fine of $20 and costs would be about right. And this fine and costs were ordered in the matter. Jessie Carroll was not pleased with this disposition of the matter, as she says she has proof positive of the stealing, and Blanche did not assault her, and the grand jury did not indict her for assault. She thinks 'law is a queer thing.'

It would be interesting to know the true facts of the above story. Jessie Carroll's observation would appear to be valid. More money was probably spent on train tickets between Silverton and Durango then the assessed fine. Did Blanche pay off the District Attorney and the Judge with money or favors? The answer to this question will never be known. A week after the trial, evil Blanche received justice from a horse. The September 27, 1884, _Silverton Democrat_ printed the following article:

Blanche DeVille, one of the Blair Street doves, was out riding with her lover Tuesday evening and met with quite a painful accident. In returning to town from Howardsville it seems that her saddle turned and she was thrown violently to the ground. Her left collar bone was broken in two places. The fractured member was set by Drs. Brown and Presby and she is said to be doing very well at present.

After her accident, nothing more was heard from Blanche. She probably decided to move on to greener pastures.

"IRISH" NELL, "DUTCH" LENA, "OREGON SHORT LINE", AND MINNIE, "THE BABY JUMBO"

These delicate lasses created quite a stir on early-day Blair Street. The first mention of their gentle nature was printed in the March 27, 1886, _La Plata Miner_ :

CHAPTER SEVEN

Two members of the demi monde engaged in a fracas at Jane Bowen's saloon on Wednesday night, which will probably culminate in the next term of the district court, to be held here next month. It appeared that one of the women, who is known to the frequenters of Blair Street as "Dutch Lena" has been for some time lying upon a bed of sickness, but has recently recovered. During Dutch Lena's sickness another frail one, who revels under the sobriquet of 'Irish Nell' had been circulating stories about the other which has roused that lady's righteous indignation. On her convalescence, Lena immediately set out and camped upon the trail of her traducer, and they finally met on the evening in question at the saloon above referred to. No time was lost in commencing a heated discussion, and one word brought on another until Dutch Lena snatched up a beer glass and struck Irish Nell in the face, cutting a fearful gash on her lower lip. The woman ran out on the street yelling at the top of her voice, and startling the classic shades of that portion of town with her cries of agony. The night watchman, arrested Dutch Lena and locked her up. Dr. Pascoe was called to attend the injured woman, and the following day when the hearing was set, the doctor stated that it would be dangerous for Irish Nell to attend the trial. The preliminary examination is set for 3 o'clock this afternoon. It will probably be a case for the grand jury. Dutch Lena was admitted to bail. 'Dutch' Lena's real name was Lena Windsor.

Note: The March 22 paper stated that: "Dutch Lena was discharged from custody on Thursday, the grand jury having failed to find an indictment."

"Irish" Nell's lip had barely healed when the two above doves along with "Minnie, The Baby Jumbo" attacked one of their erstwhile competitors, "Oregon Short Line." The June 19, 1886, *Silverton Standard* called the fight:

'Oregon Short Line', is the euphonious alias of a lady of easy virtue, who constitutes a portion of the broadgauge system of Blair Street. Her carrying capacity was severely tested Tuesday night, in fact she was overloaded with wormy prunes and sour beer. 'Irish' Nell, 'Dutch' Lena and Minnie, 'the baby Jumbo,' all three creatures with a firm foothold on aboel (sic) were on the warpath, spoiling for a fight. When Short Line came to the front as in the language of a by stander of French extraction, the three ladies 'got do vone d— sutis fi.' They double teamed on the Short Line and made it quite interesting for her for a few minutes. The scene of the accident was at the Alhambra on Blair Street (Present site of the "Green" House) The expense to the belligerents was, several black eyes, torn and disarranges costumes and $5 and trimmings assessed by his Honor, Police Justice Boyle.

Note: The French phrase is not translatable as written.

JIMMIE-THE-TOUGH

The turn of the century introduced a new name to Silverton harlotry, "Jimmie-the-Tough." She, like many of her counterparts, made the news because of her crude and violent nature. The February 23, 1901, *Silverton Standard* printed the following account of Jimmie's action:

Friday morning Jimmie-the-Tough, alias Fly Frankie, was arraigned before the bar of justice charged with having used obscene and threatening language to Miss Polka Derick, colored. Both ladies were pure as they were virtuous and virtuous as they were pure. Plaintiff told her story in a plain straightforward manner, totally unvarnished by untruthful technicality. Defendant came back at the dark damsel with an attempt to checkmate. 'Ladies, I'm sorry' volunteered His Honor, 'and more so, because its the birthday of our glorious Washington and should be venerated with an unobtrusive tank, minus combustibles. No doubt that both of you were to blame, because a fuss never originated with one person alone, yet according to the evidence elicited, I find Miss Jimmie guilty of the awful crime of obscenity, allied with that of threatening to crack Miss Derrick's coconut, and in pursuance thereof, Miss Jimmie, I shall be obliged to charge you up with $5 and costs, total amounting to $21.05. Officer Morris take charge of the prisoner until the fine is paid. Ladies good day.'

A year later, on August 2, 1902, Jimmie made the news again. This time the *Standard* printed:

Harry Morris, another youngster who is going the pace, was read the riot act to the tune of $5 and costs Wednesday afternoon for fighting. As none of the prisoners had the wherewithal with which to settle their fines, they were put upon a bread and water diet and yesterday the male offenders were organized into a chain gang and are now doing duty on the streets. Mrs. Morris was assigned the job of scrubbing the jail.

The new Mrs. Harry Morris, otherwise known as "Jimmie-the Tough," was fined $5 and costs at the same time and for the same offense that jarred her living husband.

A few months later, Jimmie was involved in a shooting scrape in Durango. The November 15, 1902, _Standard_ printed the following article:

> Frank Tell, better known in Silverton as 'Dutch Jake,' got into a shooting scrape over 'Jimmie-the-Tough' at Durango Tuesday night. Jake proved to be a poor marksman after a few trials. His target was Policeman Alexander who refused to return the fire at first for fear of hitting innocent people who were in the range of his gun. When he started in Jake threw away his gun and made for 'tall timber' but was captured and thrown in jail.

The above women were only a small part of the life of Blair Street. Many stories were printed in the local newspapers about the weekly arrests and fines of the army of whores and Madames that gave the descriptive adjective "notorious" to Blair Street.

---

[17] The National Hall was located on the southeast corner of 12th and Blair streets, adjacent to where the train stops.

CHAPTER EIGHT
THOSE BATTLING "LADIES"

As was stated in the last chapter, fighting was one of the specialties of the ladies of the night. The combatants were usually two "girls" fighting over a man or fights between the "soiled doves" and their customers. The August 27, 1892, _Silverton Standard_ documents the following:

> "A fallen angel known as P. Jenny had an altercation with a miner on Tuesday. Jenny received several cuts on the head and is in charge of the doctor. The assailant ornaments the town jail."

These miners were rough lovers and developed incredible arm muscles from swinging a four-pound hammer for ten hours a day in the mines. The November 10, 1900, _Standard_ printed the results of a love bout: "One of the dance hall force of sirens had an arm broken Wednesday night. Accident, good natured scuffle with her lover."

CHAPTER EIGHT

Many of the more serious fights were instigated by jealous men when they found their favorites with other men. An example of the latter was printed in the November 15, 1890, _Silverton Standard_ and read as follows:

> Charles Hill played a one day's engagement at the court and contributed $16.50 for striking E. L. Roberts. Like all quarrels there was a woman at the bottom of it, someone named Highland Mary, but we are not acquainted with her. But the case which took the most time and the most legal talent was a complaint filed by Charles Mader, charging Mary Paxton and Carrie Wilson, two damsels, who for a consideration disregarded the seventh commandment, with robbing him of seventy dollars. The trial lasted all day and the girls were discharged.

An example of plain old fashioned temper resulted in the following near-fatal encounter:

March 27, 1897, _Silverton Standard_:

> Tuesday afternoon there occurred at the Silver Moon Restaurant an event that very narrowly missed being a killing. Three sporting women of Blair Street were entertaining friends at the above named restaurant, which is kept by Dave Barry. They were getting boisterous and Mr. Barry, in trying to restore order, offended one of the girls, known as Flossy, who retaliated by using very strong language. A short time following the departure of the crowd of feasters, Flossy came back to the restaurant, went into the kitchen, where she found Barry and made a vicious lunge at him with a small dagger. Barry threw up his hands and caught the weapon by its sharp blade and in the struggle which ensued for the possession of the weapon all but the first finger of the hand were cut to the bone. Dr. Prewitt was called and sewed up the wounds from which no serious consequences are anticipated. Flossy was ejected from the premises and subsequently arrested in the dance hall where she works and gave bonds for appearance before the Police Court at three o'clock Wednesday where she pleaded guilty and was fined $5 and costs ($12.05).

It would be interesting to know what one would have to do in Silverton to receive a $10 fine.

The April 28, 1900, _Silverton Standard_ reported the following jealous spat:

THOSE BATTLING "LADIES"

"TEN DAY" SHOOTS JOHN LAMBERT TWICE
But Without Fatal Results.

At 10:30 o'clock Monday night those in the vicinity of the 'Hub" saloon were startled by the report of five shots in quick succession and upon inquiry the following report of the affair was learned:

It seems as if Jack Turner, known as 'Ten Day Jack,' had won the affections of a girl, a late arrival from Denver, by the name of Blanche, and for the past week they were at outs. About 10 o'clock Jack was informed that his girl was with Lambert and he, Lambert, was about to capture the fair damsel. Turner at once left the 'Hub' and upon his return he discovered the couple at the bar drinking. Without saying a word he went back through the gate at the upper end of the bar and at once began firing over the bar at Lambert and the girl, Blanche. Five shots were fired from a six-shooter, known as a 38 on a 45 frame, two of the shots taking effect in the right side about two inches under the arm, the balls passing through the fleshy part circling around the ribs and coming out at the front, no bones being broken. Lambert at once went to Dr. Ingersoll's office where the wounds were dressed.

Ten Day walked out of the front door of the saloon going directly to Lillie Reed's house on Blair Street and opened the door, advancing toward the girl, striking her over the head with the gun he previously used in the shooting, inflicting two slight wounds.

Jack's whereabouts were unknown during the night as the night watch and others failed to locate him, but on the following morning, he gave himself up to the sheriff.

So far as doing anything to surpress this kind of business the night watch will report that he counted the shots—ince, swi, tri, fer, fin.

At the present time Lambert has so far recovered as to be able to leave his room.

REPORT ON THE SHOOTING

They say Doud was playing a heart solo and at the first shot, grabbed the Queen of Hearts, and escaped with her through the back door, up the alley, around the block and came back claiming the game.

Johnnie Dettines was riveted to the spot, until after the third shot, when he made two jumps and landed in the wine room without a scratch.

Herman Strobel tried to climb the water pipe line.

'San Juan Jimmy' being down stairs at the rear of the building was the first to discover the noise of the shots.

CHAPTER EIGHT

King, the barber, after listening to the sweet song of the first bullet, took a header under the faro layout.

'Joe' fainted dead away and in that condition pulled a card table over on top of himself.

Ross ducked.

A big Swede crawled under the wine room door and went through the alley window.

The Editor of this paper who was on the spot for the express purpose of chronicling the item never moved from his seat but was cool and collected throughout the whole affair notwithstanding other assertions to the contrary.

All of the above gentlemen paid dearly for the above encounter. "Ten Day Jack" was found guilty and sentenced to the state penitentiary at Canon City. The paper stated that his name would be changed to "Ten Year Jack" if he didn't behave himself in prison.

John Lambert's wife filed for divorce and won an alimony settlement to accompany his two bullet holes.

Shortly after this incident, the Night Watchman was instructed to arrest any and all women found in the main part of saloons before the hour of midnight and after 6 o'clock in the morning.

The conditions on Blair Street were so bad by May of 1900, that the residents who owned homes south of Tenth Street petitioned the city council to change the name of the street, from 10th Street south, to Empire Street. The petition was granted. At a later time, after the prostitution and gambling ceased, the entire street was changed to Empire Street and actually retains that name today. Blair Street is a historical name.

Meanwhile the fighting continued. The May 26, 1900, _Silverton Standard_ reported:

A four-handed fight made the night hideous on the bowery last Tuesday evening. Nightwatch Behrman also took a part in the melee and was knocked down. The participants of the fight were Minnie Williams and Elsie Leslie, parties of the first part, who received a penalty

THOSE BATTLING "LADIES"

of $13.10 each for their wrong doing and Louis Borg and Joe Calava, parties of the second part, received respectively $13.10 and $33.00, Joe having gone one better by tackling the officer of the law, who was trying to separate the combatants.

About a month later, the paper reported:

May Fisher and Frankie Ford, two misguided damsels from Blair Street were brought before his Honor Thursday afternoon on a charge of having a 'battle royal' and were assessed the usual amount—'$5 and costs daughters.'

One of the problems with keeping peace and order on Blair Street, or any other street, was the tendency of miners to be hard drinkers. Most of the incidents of violence were the result of too much booze. The December 8, 1900, *Standard* printed:

At 2 o'clock Wednesday afternoon, George Lynch was arraigned before the bar of justice, charged with having inflicted several smashes on the head of Miss Sidney Davis, of Blair Street, and also having smashed a mirror belonging to that lady to smithereens. From the testimony it appears that Mr. Lynch was drunk on the occasion, therefore, His Honor placed the penalty in moderation—$10 and costs, which included the price of the looking glass—total $36.85.

The September 6, 1902, issue of the *Standard* printed two accounts of violence among the Blair Street inhabitants:

Monday afternoon an employee at the Silver Lake (Mine) approached a Blair Street woman and after an altercation with her grabbed her purse containing about $80 and ran with it. The officers had a very meager description of the miscreant, but finally located the right person and captured him Tuesday morning. But his friends came to his rescue, the money was refunded and the woman refused to prosecute, the fellow was turned loose.

Police Court News:

It was slightly cool in the court room the morning of the 3rd and Judge Hodges was not feeling his best when Pearl Marshall, alias 'Gip' stepped before the altar of justice (by request) and pleaded guilty to a charge of fighting. Pearl winked one eye (the other was too black to budge) and the judge said 'total $14.75.'

Louise Maurell was called next to answer the same charge and with an assuring air said 'not guilty.' The judge would not stand for the bluff and said '$10 and costs, full amount $19.75.' Louise requested that she be confined in a secluded spot owned by the city. While on her way to the bastille, Louise changed her mind and donated the sum to the city funds.

The April 11, 1903, *Standard* contained a brief comment on another of the fair ladies: "Gipsy" Brown paid as fine and costs $24.65 this week. Fighting and disturbing the peace." A week later, the April 18, 1903, paper printed:

> In a row at one of the dance halls last Tuesday night, B. F. Hall was severely cut about the head and face. On the following day Hall swore out a warrant charging Romeo Snyder with doing the cutting and the latter was arrested and his hearing set for this afternoon before Judge Watson.

"Romeo," was sentenced to the county jail for a short stay. With a name like that he must have been a hit in the bordellos.

A month later, "Broken-nose Grace" was fined $5 and costs in police court Wednesday for "conduct entirely unbecoming most people's idea of a lady."

The June 18, 1904, issue of the *Standard* printed the story of another attack by a man on one of the women. The size of the fine was dependent upon the amount of damage that was done to the person of the woman:

> Charles Ellenbert, a cook at the Royal Restaurant, who was arrested on the charge of assault and battery on the person of Miss Emma Burns of Blair Street, and at the urgent request of His Honor, washed his guilty sins away by the payment of $25 and costs, total amount aggregating $49.50. (This was about a month's pay.)

It was obvious that the editor of the *Silverton Standard* considered all of these encounters with the Blair Street women as a joke. He seemed to relish using his eloquent writing style in describing these breaches of the peace. The following is a classic example:

January 7, 1905, *Silverton Standard*:

> Two Finns were arrested Tuesday night, namely Hjalmar Nyquist and Gus Gustafson, for disturbing the peace and quietude of a soiled

THOSE BATTLING "LADIES"

dove on Blair Street. They were brought before Squire Watson the following day, and although there was no evidence against Gus Gustafson, the Squire fined him $5 and costs. Nyquist received the same dose, but it is believed he deserved it on general principles. The harrowed feelings of the pigeon were soothed, the Squire makes $13 clear, and the Finns will play checkers with their noses at the city sweat house.

Since the above was put in type Gus Gustafson has been pardoned, and rightfully, too, by the mayor.

Most of the prostitutes who worked in cribs were independent and depended upon pimps to bring their customers to them. These men, for the most part, were from the lowest rung on the ladder of humanity. Physical abuse of the girls by these bullies was not uncommon. The December 9, 1905, *Silverton Standard* reported the actions of one Frank Anderson. It is not known for certain whether Frank Anderson was a pimp or just a bully, but the paper put him in the same class as a pimp:

One day the past week Frank Anderson, a waiter known as 'Pancake Frank,' got belligerent and went on the warpath. Being an arrant, cowardly bully, he jumped onto 'his girl,' Mable Kelly, a dance hall artist, and beat her up in a most brutal manner, knocking her down and punching and kicking her into insensibility. The victim of the brutal assault was taken to the hospital where she has hovered between life and death ever since. It is thought now that the girl will recover. Anderson was arrested and is now in jail awaiting trial and the outcome of the girl's injuries. He should be given the limit of the law, and when he has served his sentence he should be hot-footed out of camp. In case of his return he should be given a good substantial coat of tar and feathers. There is entirely too many affairs of this kind happening in Silverton. It is bad enough for men to be 'laying up' with these women of the half-world, but these disgraceful affairs where big husky brutes, too cowardly to fight men, get into fights with and beat up weak, defenseless women, should be put a stop to, and that too, speedily and effectively. And in this connection, it may fittingly be added that there are a number of self-alleged men in this town who are living off the gains from the shame of women, who should be given a good hasty start down the canyon, with an emphatic warning to keep on going and not let the foolish idea of coming back enter their heads.

Such was the glamorous life of early-day Silverton prostitutes.

CHAPTER 9
POTPOURRI

THE TOWN HALL

By 1910, Blair Street had reached its peak. Very few vacant lots existed between 11th and 13th streets. Not every building was a bordello. A few were saloons and boarding houses for miners. Until 1909, the Silverton Town Hall was sandwiched between a bordello called the Stone Saloon, and a small building which served as a crib. The townfolks were constantly clamoring for a new city hall located away from Blair Street. "Proper" women would not be seen near Blair Street and this made things a little inconvenient when they had business at the town hall. This, however, was not always the case. During the early years of Silverton, the "society" people would often attend variety shows and dances on Blair Street. The early dance halls, such as Jane Bowen's, were the scenes of social dances in which the entire town was invited. The town hall was also used for gala events. The January 9, 1886, *Silverton Democrat* wrote with disgust about the fusion of the two social elements in an article entitled:

TWO BALLS IN ONE NIGHT

We have seen 'ten nights in a bar room,' and ten bar rooms in a night; but last evening was the first opportunity we ever had to see two balls in the same room in one night. While we did not attend either, we are assured by parties who attended both that each was a grand success.

For the past week the Reese Ball to be given at the town hall Friday evening, January 8th, had been the talk of society circles in the city, and the turnout last evening was large and embraced the best and most highly respected element of Silverton society. The ball was in every feature a success, and, in harmony with a modest and temperate appreciation of the proprieties, the ball broke up at 1 a. m. The ladies were escorted to their moral and happy homes, and we regret to say, that in some cases their escorts returned to the ball to attend the second ball of the evening—for no sooner had the respectable element left the ball and it was taken possession of by the demi monde—and to the strains of the same music and beneath the same lights, with a change of partners, began the Bacchanalian orgies of abandoned revelry. Beneath the careluia (sic) lights, with flagrant suggestiveness, the racquet, the shadow, and the can-can were gone through to the finish.

It was between five and six o'clock this morning when ball number two ended.

The indignation of the respectable ladies of our city, who attended the first ball is just. It is an insult to them which deserves the indignant resentment of all good people. It will have a tendency to render fatal all efforts to get up a respectable social ball in the future. If it were intended for a joke, the parties who are responsible for it should be reminded that it is one which partakes of the character of an insult to every virtuous wife, mother, or sister in the city.

Fig. 14 Silverton Volunteer Fire Department in front of 1883 Silverton City Hall. San Juan County Hist. Soc. Photo.

Fig. 15 Remains of 1883 Silverton Town Hall. New false-front added in fall of 1986. Allan Bird Photo.

Fig. 16 Original doorway to 1883 Blair Street Town Hall. 1987. Allan Bird Photo.

Fig 17 1954 photo of old city hall on left. Sign painted for movie set. Building to the right is the 1897 Stone Saloon where Peter Dalla was shot. Porch added for movie set. Ruth Gregory Photo.

GAMBLING

Associated with many of the bordellos was liquor and gambling. Most of the gambling joints were rigged and the hapless miner with his hard-earned wages had little or no chance of coming out ahead. The _Silverton Democrat_ went on a crusade to warn the naive about the futility of "bucking the tiger." On April 10, 1886, they wrote:

STAY CLEAR OF THE THIEVING TINHORN

In a few weeks many of the mines that have employed from ten to fifty men during the past six months will pay off. We hope the men who have worked so long and hard to acquire a few hundred dollars will take care of their money when they get it. They should resolve not to be a picknick or pudding for a tin horn gambler. There are dozens of this class in Silverton who have lived all winter from hand to mouth but have made their boasts of having some sucker working for them in the mines, and they looked forward with bright anticipation to the day when said sucker will draw his wages for his winter's work and come to town to turn it over to said tin horn. If the honest hard-working miners will allow the tin horn gamblers to live off themselves their ranks will soon be thinned out in Silverton.

There is no gambling game at cards played in Silverton that the outsider does not have 100 percent the worst of the game, and a miner or laborer who plays against them never has been known to win and they never will win, and he who is fool enough to risk his money where the odds are against him to such a great extent as they are in any game in Silverton, ought not to win. We hope the miner who is in any danger of losing his winters wages at the gaming tables, will, before he draws his wages provide some safe investment or place for his money where he will proceed to place it as soon as it is paid over to him. Steer clear of thieving tin horns.

CHAPTER NINE

THE DO-GOODERS

The W.C.T.U. (Women's Christian Temperance Union) entered Silverton in 1890. By March of that year the organization listed fourteen members. They originally met once a month but decided that to keep up with the sin in Silverton they would meet every two weeks. There was actually fear in town that Carrie Nation, the hatchet-swinging saloon reformer, would attack the saloons of Silverton. She had made a shambles of bar rooms across Kansas.

As Silverton became more "civilized" over the years, an active core of reformers developed and put pressure on the local authorities to clean up Blair and Greene streets. They met violent opposition from the miners and the mine owners. After a miner worked seven days a week for four or five months without a break, his mental health would become questionable. Fights would break out in the mines and the boarding houses. A good mine superintendent could judge when a man was ready to "blow in," a term used for rest and rehabilitation. When severe cabin fever set in, the superintendent would order the miner to town with instructions "not to return until he was $300 in debt." This would assure the mine owners of a constant work force as the men could not afford to quit. The large majority of the miners were young and single. The town fathers liked the influx of miners spending their money as it provided a steady source of revenue for the town coffers.

For a short time in the early history of Silverton, the forces of good won over the forces of evil and in the spring of 1897, the good people of Silverton actually did make an attempt to enforce the ordinance against gambling. They also made a concerted effort to evict the bums and pimps. On July 26, 1897, the hammer of respectability fell on Silverton. The July 31 issue of the *Silverton Standard* printed the following notice along with the heated arguments going around town on the pros and cons of gambling:

POTPURRI

GAMBLING CLOSED

Last Monday about 4 o'clock, Sheriff Hines went around to the different houses where gambling was being carried on and notified the proprietors that they must cease operations. There was a great deal of kicking, but the command was obeyed and by 6 o'clock nearly every gambler in the city was looking over the map of the Klondike and inquiring about the price of transportation to Durango. Some venture to remark that it is the last of gambling in Silverton, while others think that it will soon blow over and amount to naught.

PROS AND CONS OF GAMBLING

To the Standard:

Has it become necessary to make Silverton a 'Sunday Town'? I believe the enjoyment is limited to a too small scope, our natural resources does not permit of boulevards, parks, or road houses, etc., and why the pent up sporting houses should now be closed, by a few, through a selfish motive, is beyond my understanding. Does prohibition prohibit gambling? Does not the miner who it is stated, is muchly abused by this business, seek some place to vent his desirous western disposition, there is some cellar, attic, or even adjoining rooms to saloons, chance his luck for wheel or woe? Whenever the same role of strict morality, prevalent in the east is applied to a mining camp, it is time to move. Men are natural gamblers as will be evinced at even our church raffles. It does look as if the whole scheme was preconcocted by a few for personal benefit, and it is a poor rule that does not work both ways: if gambling is closed in saloons, why not close gambling in other buildings under whatever auspices the same may be conducted, whether it be the dice box on the cigar case, the nickel-in-the-slot machine, or the "Holy of Holy" that starts you to guessing whether or not you are justified in spending your money on a game of chance at a church gathering. I believe that the closing of gambling is a detriment to any live western town, for when men spend money before the eyes of capitalists who are seeking investments they (the capitalists) have not been disappointed in finding the 'wild and woolly' west other than had been represented. They realize that the mountains in the vicinity must yield this lustful gold. Now here comes a rub, a rub that these saintly kickers will open their eyes too soon. At present property within the corporate limits is not taxed, for reasons, that the saloons and gambling houses have heretofore paid the taxes sufficient to defray the expenses of the city government. Not only this they have placed in the city coffers, a handsome sum to boot. A tax will soon have to be levied. I trust that this clinch as 'the ungodly' will be of short durations—Yours respectfully,
Rep.

CHAPTER NINE

To The Editor of the Standard:

Dear Sir:

I gladly comply with your request, to give for your paper a few of the reasons why everyone should take a stand against gambling. But first let us see what the two stock arguments are worth, that its advocates are continually trotting out. The first is, that 'Gambling puts money in circulation.' True, but the mere circulation is nothing. When a miner receives his earnings and spends the money for his family to pay the grocer and marketman, the carpenter and painter for improving his house, and his taxes, and then deposits his savings in the bank against a rainy day, that is the kind of circulation that helps the community. But when the burglars blew open the safe at the sampler and stole the money it was put in circulation but I doubt if anyone will claim that such circulation is of any benefit to the community. And gambling stands on just the same plane. One loses and the winner has what he never earned and has no right to. Such circulation helps no one. The second argument is 'If men can't gamble here they will go the Durango.' Well so much the worse for the men and for Durango. One man might be such a fool while ten would help Silverton by what they spent and saved here. This is like the excuse the horsethief gave that 'If he had not stolen the horse another man would.' And perhaps Durango may be decent some day too. But there are higher arguments. Gambling is against the laws of God, the state and our conscience, and no one who respects God, the state or himself will gamble; and he who does will have to pay the penalty. He may escape the state, but God and himself he can never escape. Think of the homes that have been destroyed, and the young men ruined by this vice. I have attended the funerals of too many suicides to forget that. And the poor professional gambler comes to be a mere parasite on the honest labor of the community. The food he eats, the clothes he wears, the roof that shelters him are all the product of the toil of others. Instead of helping in the struggle for life, he takes the food from the children's mouths, and the clothing from the wife and mother, and no wonder they lose their higher manhood. Many of then are kind and generous and some of my personal friends, yet there are few more to be pitied, for their business is their ruin, and many have no other means of living. In short gambling is a sin against God, a crime against the state, and wrong against self, the family and the community. It is utterly selfish and inhuman. The result is all evil. It simply has no excuse.

The cure of this evil is in the home. The children should be taught the dignity of labor and the sin and disgrace of idleness. There should be no gambling in the home. A mother remonstrated with her son who had been winning money at poker. He pointed to a vase on the mantle saying 'Mother, how did you get that?' 'Oh' said the mother embarrased,

'I won that at whist.' 'Very well,' said the son, you play for prizes and I play for money, its all the same thing.' And too any church that raises money by lotteries and grab bags can do more to teach the children gambling than all the faro banks in the city.

Hoping your readers will give this subject their most serious thought I am—Yours truly, W. T. Jordan (Pastor of People's Church)

Of the three vices,—liquor, gambling, and prostitution; gambling lost for at least a week. The exact length of the prohibition is not known but before long the town was back in full swing. Perhaps the property tax threat of the backers of sin turned the tide.

THE CHINESE "PROBLEM"

Prejudice against the Chinese came to a head on Blair Street. For years the Chinese operated laundries and restaurants in Silverton. The newspapers of the day always attached the descriptive adjectives of, "pig-tailed, almond-eyed celestials" or similar derogatory terms when writing of the Chinese. For the most part, the Chinese were extremely hard-working industrious people. Because of their religious beliefs they were referred to as heathens. The introduction of opium joints to Silverton was their main drawback.  Many of the women on Blair Street took to the "pipe," to relieve their dreary existence.

About the turn of the century, after the formation of the labor unions, things came to a head in Silverton. The unions published a hate letter in the February 8, 1902, _Silverton Standard_ ordering the townfolks to boycott all Chinese establishments. The letter read as follows:

CHAPTER NINE

APPEAL TO THE PEOPLE

Do you want the yellow man or the white man? We, as organized labor ask the people of Silverton and San Juan County for their full support in regards to the Chinese question, which is a serious question to be considered.

As citizens they are a failure; they do not assimilate as citizens and their habits are so obnoxious that they become the most undesirable class of people in the community in which they reside. The opium habit, which has destroyed thousands of lives, is ready to destroy more if not checked. The Chinese dens in this city have destroyed over three hundred human beings. How long are you going to stand this? Is it not time to do something while the evil is yet in its infancy?

No white man can compete with their labor on account of their cheapness in living. Who reaps the benefit from them? Does the tailor or barber, or the butcher and grocer? The butcher and grocer may at present, but let them increase and where are you? Look at San Francisco, California, and Portland, Oregon. Beware! This is a warning for the future. Why not be men and act as such? Look at Cripple Creek, Leadville and Colorado Springs. Why don't they have Chinese? Are we not the same kind of men, or are we weaklings? If it were not for the powers of the world, where would the white people who are in China be today? Stop and consider this vital question. Do you want them? If not, then join us.

As we intend, THEY MUST GO.

Executive Committee
W. F. & M. No. 26.
Cooks and Waiters Union 16.
Federal Labor Union 112.

Whereas, the Chinese are a public nuisance and a detriment to the public welfare; and

Whereas, the white laborer cannot compete with the Chinese labor; therefore, be it

Resolved, that we, the Silverton Miners Union No. 26, W. F. M., do hereby declare a boycott on all Chinese; and be it further

Resolved, that we ask all union men and fair-minded citizens to withdraw their patronage from all Chinamen.

All but a few of the Chinese packed up and left for Durango or Ouray. Several had built businesses which had been in operation for years. One man by the name of W. S. Hung, owned a small wooden shack located on the east side of Blair Street about midway between 11th and 12th streets. He opened his small laundry in 1894, which became known as "Spiders". He did much of the laundry for the "soiled doves" of Blair Street and was well accepted until the unions bullied the population into following their boycott. On the night of May 12, 1902, a mob of angry whites decided to drive the last Chinaman out of Silverton. As the mob approached W. S. Hung's small home and laundry, he panicked and fired two shots through the door in an effort to stop them from entering. The mob returned the fire with three shots. The paper's comment that, "this Chinaman did not accompany the crowd," would indicate that they had murdered him. In May of that year W. S. Hung issued a quit claim deed to Jack Slattery for his property. Perhaps it was another man that fired the shots and was in turn shot. The remainder of the Chinese were rounded up and ropes put around their necks. Terrified that they were about to be lynched, they were led out of town to the entrance of the canyon. There they were released and ordered to "hike." One or two of them, who were well liked in the past, persuaded the mob to let them return and at least sell their property and retain their possessions.

Fig. 18 W. S. Hung's Chinese Laundry, known as "Spider's." where armed mob drove the Chinese out of Silverton in 1902. Late 1883 Photo. Fattor's Tremount Saloon and Bordello built on this site in 1907. Colo. Hist. Soc. Photo.

THE
AUSTRIAN-ITALIAN INVASION

During the 1890's and the first decade of the twentieth century, strong ethnic transitions took place in Silverton. In the early days, the bulk of the population was of English or Irish descent. The heavy influx of Cornish miners from southern England helped open the San Juans as a premier-class mining district. The English, Irish, and Scotch were followed by the Swedish and Finnish miners. During the construction of the Red Mountain railroad, trainloads of Italians were imported. After completion of the railroad, many of these men remained in Silverton and worked in the mines. Actually, many of the so-called Italians were actually Austrians from the province of Tyrol, which after World War 1 became part of northern Italy. The actual natives of Italy came, for the most part, from the northern part of Italy, namely the provinces of Piemonte and Tuscany. From the very beginning, there was a rivalry between the Tyroleans and the Piemontes; sometimes friendly, sometimes violent. Twelfth Street became the dividing line. For the most part, the Tyroleans lived and had their businesses on Blair Street south of 12th. The Piemontes lived north of 12th. By the early 1900's, almost every saloon and bordello on Blair Street was owned and operated by this ethnic group.

Trouble erupted in May of 1904 when Peter Dalla, whose real name was Dallapicola, was shot by Barney Fori. Dalla, a Tyrolean, was courting the daughter of the late Louis Sartore, a Piemonte. Mrs. Sartore owned the Bellview saloon, now Zhivago's Restaurant, and was dead set against her daughter marrying Dalla. Rumor had it that Mrs. Sartore hired Fori to kill Dalla. This was never proven. On the night of May 16, 1904, the *Silverton Standard* printed the following story, which occurred in the Stone Saloon:[18]

POTPURRI

SERIOUS FRACTURE

*Sustained in the Shooting Scrape Last
Saturday Evening*

'Throw up your hands.' was the command of Barney Fori who entered the rear door of the Stone Saloon, Blair Street, at 11:30 last Saturday evening. Pointing from his right hand was the long, shining barrel of a 44- Colts revolver, and this little weapon served as a persuader of much more than average power. Most hands went up, but whether those of Pete Dalla, one of the proprietors of the place, did or not, this reporter was unable to learn. At any rate Mr. Dalla became the victim of the intruder who fired two shots, one of which took effect in his left leg just above the knee, passing through the leg and shattering the bone in a most frightful manner.

Mr. Dalla was standing near the bar at the time of the shooting and fell to the floor unable to move. His assailant at once fled from the scene of his crime and was captured a little later by Officer Morris who had heard the shots and was on hand to acquire a description of the man and details of the shooting. The prisoner was taken to the county jail and placed behind bars for safe keeping.

Several persons were present when the shooting occurred and when they saw Dalla fall, seriously injured, they at once summoned Dr. Fox who had the wounded man removed to his room, where necessary surgical attention was given, and the patient is now reported as resting well and chances are favorable for his complete recovery without leaving him a permanent cripple.

The exact cause of the shooting is not known though many theories have been advanced. It is known, however, that Messrs. Dalla and Fori were not on friendly terms. In the early part of the evening Fori entered the saloon and as he passed Dalla he made the remark. 'I'll get you yet.' He proceeded through the door and shortly after returned and ordered 'hands up,' after which the shooting occurred. Mr. Dalla, it is said, was to have wedded a certain well known young lady of the city on Sunday, and that it was Fori's infatuation for this same young lady which created a desire for the removal of his rival.

Police Court:
Barney Fori fined $50 and trimmings, the sum total being $59.75. Barney was not in possession of the amount demanded and in consequence accepted the only alternative—a limited season behind the bars of the county jail.

CHAPTER NINE

The following week, Barney Fori was bound over to the district court in the sum of $1000. Failing to secure the bond, he was placed in the county jail until the September term of the court. Before September he was released.

Peter Dalla's wedding had been scheduled for the week after he was shot but his leg wound turned out to be much more serious than originally thought. By September his leg had healed enough to reschedule his wedding. The week before his wedding, on September 15, 1904, Peter Dalla was murdered in a most brutal manner. The September 17, 1904, *Silverton Standard* printed the story in vivid detail:

INSTANT DEATH

Came To Peter Dalla in a Terrific Explosion

Residents of this city and particularly those residing on East 13th near Blair and Mineral streets were awakened at 3:30 Thursday morning by a terrific explosion, and as they hastily arose from their couches, grave fears were entertained of some dreadful disaster.

In a very few moments the streets were thoroughly crowded with anxious persons seeking the scene of wreckage and possible blood-shed. All were headed for a point between Blair and Mineral and here found the little frame cottage occupied by Peter Dalla with the north side almost blown out, the interior furnishings badly wrecked and the lifeless body of Dalla deposited in the opposite side of the room from where the explosion occurred.

A thorough examination of the premises revealed the fact that several sticks of Giant Powder (dynamite) had been suspended on the outer wall of the building and near the head of Dalla's bed. All being satisfactorily placed and the intended victim fast asleep, the combustibles were ignited in some unknown manner with the result above given. So great was the force of the explosion that a building adjoining that occupied by Dalla was also badly wrecked—doors blown off, frame work splintered, windows shattered and furnishings demolished. Fortunately no one was in the cottage at the time or other victims would have been registered.

There is no absolute clue to the murderer of Mr. Dalla, since no one but the perpetrator of this dastardly deed seems to have been witness to the explosion, and yet there is little doubt in the minds of officers and friends of the victim who recall details of an attempt on Dalla's life at 11 o'clock on Saturday night May 14 last by Barney Fori, and this same man, it is reported, has made numerous threats since.

Standard readers will doubtless remember the assault upon Dalla by Fori in the former's saloon on Blair Street. Fori entered the place through a rear door and, with a Colts revolver pointed at persons present, commanded all hands to go up. Two shots were fired at Dalla, one taking effect in his left leg just above the knee.

The ill will existing between Dalla and Fori is said to have arisen from the infatuation of each for the same girl. Dalla was successful in his suit for the hand of this fair young maiden and twice has a date been set for the ceremony uniting their lives, but as many times has their purpose been thwarted. This time the affair is forever cancelled by death of the successful suitor.

Fori was found at Animas Forks by officer Walter Campbell. He was in bed partly dressed. He was arrested and is now behind bars in the county jail.

Eight witnesses were present to testify, one of the most important being Florence Baker, an employee of one of the Blair Street dance halls, who had seen the two men in the alley near Dalla's room between the hours of one and three o'clock Thursday morning. She was taken to the county jail but could not identify Fori as being one of the parties seen in the alley. The shift boss at the mine where Fori works could not be had at this hearing but it is thought he will prove a valuable witness.

September 24, 1904, *Silverton Standard*:

Tuesday night an Austrian decided to make a target of John Fori, an Italian, but missed his mark. The same evening Pete Ray, night watchman at the Gold King Office, was shot at twice, one ball passing through his coat sleeve and the other close to his head. Ray says that two men stepped up near him when he was unlocking the front door of the office and without a word one of the parties shot twice and both ran down the road toward the D. & R. G. depot. There are too few arrests made for the carrying of concealed weapons these days and a general roundup would be beneficial to the public in general and incidentally to the town treasury.

No further evidence, unless possessed by the secret detective society, has been obtained as to the party or parties implicated in the killing of Peter Dalla by dyna-mite last week. Barney Fori, the suspect is in jail and awaits a preliminary hearing. A feud of long standing between the Italian and Austrian elements of Silverton may have some bearing on the matter but to date no positive proof has been obtained.

Barney Fori was never convicted of the crime and the crime was never solved. In 1987, during a book signing party of the first edition of this book, I met the grandson of Mrs. Sartore's sister. This gentleman, a man in his 70's, said that grandma's sister, the intended brides mother, did the dastardly deed. The location of the building in which Dalla was killed was next door, to the south, of Zhivago's Restaurant. The land and building was owned by the Sartores.

VENEREAL DISEASE

During the 1920's and 1930's, Silverton became very conscious of health and sanitation on Blair Street. For some unknown reason, venereal disease was extremely rare in Silverton. By 1920, the prostitutes were well regulated. They were required to visit City Hall every month and pay their "fines" of from $10 to $25. They were also required to visit a doctor every week for a checkup. The late Ernest Hoffman related the following story about early day Blair Street:

My dad bought a boarding house in Silverton (The old Silverton Hotel) in the early 1900's and boarded only miners. He lost his butt because the boarding house was the last place the miners paid. As soon as they hit town they would head for Blair Street and blow all their money on gambling and women. As for the women, they were a social necessity in those days. You've got to remember that almost all of the miners in those days were young and single. After spending three or four months up at that mine they just had to get away for a break. Of course they never got past Silverton. Silverton was wide open with gambling and women 24 hours a day. There were a lot of 'do-gooders' in town that wanted to do away with the women but Joe Terry and the other mine managers fought to keep them. It was important that the men remained in good spirits and the gambling and women served this purpose.

As for disease among the women, I never knew of anyone getting a dose of syphilis or any other venereal disease. They were very strict about sanitation and the girls had to be checked at least once a week.

Each girl had her certificate hung on the wall, just like a college diploma. We had a Dr. Lynch who checked them each week. For awhile we had a guy named Dr. Bryant, he didn't last too long. He would go to the girl's place of business and check them out. Of course the girls all knew when he was there and they would get themselves all cleaned up and always pass the tests. Dr. Lynch made them come to his office and wait at least an hour before he checked them.

After Prohibition came, the gals sold bootleg booze along with the bars. The city fathers soon got wise to the fact that this was a ripe source of revenue. Each bootlegger and girl on the line had to come in each month and pay a set fine. That's how all those cement sidewalks in Silverton were built. The girls could only go to Main Street (Greene Street) to shop and pick up their mail. They were never allowed to linger there. One merchant that sold fine ladieswear made a fortune off of those girls.

John and Joe Matties recalled that only two or three cases of venereal disease were ever found in the Blair Street red light district during the years that they lived in Silverton. "One was a lady, and they fired her out of town fast. It was pretty safe."

Gerald Swanson found a book containing the blank health certificates issued by the town.

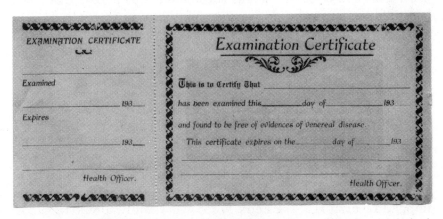

Fig. 19 San Juan County Venereal Disease Certificate issued to prostitutes on a regular basis during the 1920's and 1930's. Courtesy of Gearld Swanson.

---

18 The Stone Saloon is next door, to the south, from the present Swanee's Gift Shop located on the west side of Blair Street, south of 13th Street.

CHAPTER TEN

THE BORDELLOS, SALOONS, BOARDING HOUSES, ETC.

The two blocks between 11th and 13th streets were a conglomeration of bordellos, saloons, boarding houses and several independent businesses. The street reached its peak between 1910 and 1920. World War I caused a critical shortage of certain metals, mainly zinc, which were readily available in the San Juan Mountains. This spurred a boom in the mining industry and a heavy influx of miners, followed by the usual contingent of gamblers and prostitutes.

PROHIBITION

In 1916, Prohibition went into effect in Silverton even though national Prohibition was not enacted until January 16, 1920. Because of its relative isolation, Silverton continued to serve bootleg whiskey across the bar throughout this period. The local law enforcement officials were sympathetic to the saloons and aided in hiding the whiskey. After 1920, when word was received that the Federal Revenue agents were about to make a raid, all available hands were put to work moving the booze to a safe hiding place.

The only easy access to Silverton in the 1920's was by rail. The Durango road was not completed until October 1920 and was not kept open during the winter months. When the government agents planned a raid in Silverton, someone usually phoned ahead from Durango as soon as the train left the station, warning of the impending arrival of the Feds. Word was rapidly spread throughout town and the job of moving the liquor supplies into the Rainbow Route Garage was hastened by Town Marshal Leonard, the garage owner. Charlie Leonard also owned several of the cribs on Blair Street.

Even with the advance warning, the agents were often able to uncover stashes of bootleg whiskey and wine. One such incident was described in the February 18, 1928, *Silverton Standard*. The article read:

FIND AND DESTROY 2500 GALLONS OF WHISKEY MASH

W. E. Lukens and John Simpson, Federal enforcement officers for this district, were visitors in Silverton this week, and in going about the duties to which they were entrusted they made discoveries of several places where stills and the manufacture of intoxicants was in evidence, and when they had finished up their labors Thursday evening, they had destroyed some 2500 gallons of mash and 103 gallons of finished whiskey product.

The places that were visited were what is known as the Maple place on lower Mineral Street, the old Ben Gilbert Carpenter Shop, the Motto House on upper Blair Street, a house on 14th Street and one on 10th and Empire. In making the search of the first and third places Lukens and Simpson were aided by Marshal Leonard and Sheriff Doud.

The coming of these men was not unknown to the folks here and as a consequence much mash and other articles were hidden out by those who hold same. Mr. Lukens and Simpson say they are going to keep coming as long as they are on the job, so it will be wise for those who are in this particular line of endeavor to be watchful and careful. No disturbance was created and the coming of the men was just a matter-of-fact daily occurrence.

An interesting side note of the above raid was the destruction of Silverton's milk supply for several days. It seems that the agents dumped the confiscated mash into the local dairy's pasture and the cows feasted on the product and became thoroughly schnockered. The alcohol content was so high that the milk had to be destroyed.

Another danger of being caught selling or making bootleg whiskey was the government's practice of confiscating the furniture and fixtures of the saloons that were caught dispensing the product. The Bellview Saloon, (now Zhivago's Restaurant) had a beautiful hand-carved bar. Shortly after a successful raid, the Feds announced they would confiscate the bar and all other fixtures. Phil Sartore was the owner at the time. He knew they would be up the following day to clean him out. To preserve his beautiful bar, he hired a crew to work through the night unbolting the bar and fixtures. That night, the entire furnishings of his Bellview Saloon were moved to a safe hiding place in town. The next morning the Feds arrived and, in the words of Sartore, "They were mad as hell."

Frances Belmont's Mikado Saloon and Bordello was raided several times and the furniture confiscated. It was the practice of the government to auction off the furniture and fixtures to the highest bidder. The town folks would all band together and bid one cent on the dollar, with no one raising the bid. Often the entire auction would bring only $7 or $8. The end result was that Frances Belmont would end up with her furniture and fixtures by repaying the $7 or $8 paid by the people of Silverton.

Often the Federal agents zealous behavior would get out of hand. In one case, a young widow whose husband died in the flu epidemic of 1918 when her baby was less than two months old, was caught making and selling wine to support herself and her young son. She was arrested and sent to the federal prison for two years.

THE BORDELLOS

The largest bordellos to operate between the 1910 to 1930 period were the Laundry, so named because you were guaranteed to get "cleaned," the Diamond Belle, the Bon Ton, the Monte Carlo, the Tremount, and the National Hall. In addition to the large houses, many small establishments existed along Blair Street, such as the Tree Top, the Arcade, the Mikado, (operated by "21" Pearl and Frances Belmont), "Nigger" Lola's, "Jew" Fanny's, "Black Minnie's," "Diamond Tooth" Leona's, "Sheeny" Pearl's, Kate Starr's, Mayme Murphy's, "Tar Baby" Brown's, and many more. Several of these women operated out of the individual cribs.

THE SALOONS & BOARDING HOUSES

In addition to the bordellos, several saloons and boarding houses lined Blair Street. Among these were Matties' Welcome Saloon and Boarding House, John Giono's Saloon and Boarding House, the Bellview Saloon and Boarding House, Zanoni-Pedroni's Florence Saloon and Boarding House, Minolla's Saloon, the North Pole Saloon, and the Union House, later operated by the Tomaselli family.

After the Austrians and Italians took over Blair Street, many of the saloons built Bocci lanes beside their buildings. This was a favorite game, similar to lawn bowling, which was played on a smooth dirt alley. The Bellview, Zanoni-Pedroni's Florence and other saloons had Bocci alleys adjacent to their buildings.

THE FRENCH BAKERY

A few legitimate businesses, not related to saloons, bordellos or boarding houses, were located on Blair Street. The French Bakery, operated by Maffey and Machetto, occupied the corner next to Zhivago's Restaurant from 1909 until 1916.

This corner lot had quite a history. Tom Cain built his dance hall on this lot in 1883. After his brother Pat jumped bail, Tom was forced to turn the building over to the Town of Silverton in 1884. Silverton used it as a town office building for a short period. In 1885, a local butcher, J. W. Grow bought the lot from the city. Ten years later, the land was owned by George Bausman, a local dry goods merchant. On March 4, 1898, Bausman sold it to Ludwig Vota. Vota used it for a bordello. He also was operating Ludwig's Dance Hall, the future "Laundry". He had several other cribs on Blair Street. On May 26, 1900, Vota leased the property to Frank Alphine or Alpine. It became known as the Alpine-Sella Dance Hall.

CHAPTER TEN

In September 1901, Ludwig Vota sold the land and building to Mary Kloster. Mary Kloster and her husband leased the property to two ladies of the street, Pauline Brown and Katie King. Mary Kloster sold the property, while it was under lease to Pauline and Katie, to Ratalle Rosatti, Ben Bazzanella, Paul Tongoli, and Domenica Dallavalle. Domenica owned 2/5's and the others 3/5's. The November 12, 1904, _Silverton Standard_ printed the following account of an affray between the two girls and the former owner, Mr. Kloster:

> Last Thursday evening Pauline Brown and Katie King called on the Merchant Tailoring establishment of J. N. Kloster for the purpose of exacting a settlement of some sorts as to the possession of a license for the sale of beer in their house on Blair Street. The settlement did not satisfy the lessees of the building formerly owned by Kloster who also furnished the license, and Miss. Brown landed on him with a right swing bearing enough force to cause complete collapse. Kloster regained his equilibrium and was again sent down and out by Pauline's powerful right and the 'scrap' was ended.
>
> The duo then proceeded to have a 'good time.' Their indulgences in varied drinks caused hilarity which eventually developed into disorder and disturbance. They were arrested upon two charges, one assault and the other drunk and disorderly conduct, and in Police Court this Friday afternoon, were each fined $10 and costs. The sum total for each to drop into the city's strong box was $39.50.

On April 8, 1905, Pauline Brown applied for her own liquor license. Shortly after, she was arrested for fighting and disturbing the peace and fined the usual $14.75. In November, Katy King got into a fight with Pauline, who was the landlord of the bordello, and Katy was fined $14.75, after which she "skipped Ourayward."

By 1908, Domenica Dallavalle, Mary Swanson's mother, owned 100 percent of the property. She tore down the old dance hall and bordello and used much of the lumber to build three small shacks facing 13th Street which she rented out. Molly Foley and "Denver" Kate lived in the shack farthest from Blair Street.

Annibale Maffey and Joe Machetto purchased the property from Domenica on December 10, 1910. August Maffey and Joe Machetto were partners in the French Bakery. They started their

Fig. 20 *The Original French Bakery on the northeast corner of 13th and Blair streets showing Molly Foley's crib. Left to right: Camillo Glachetto, Joe Machetto (overalls), Celeste Motto (Baker), Joe Caffero, Barney Tocco, and Louis Cocchi—1908. Julia Maffey Photo.*

small business across the street, to the north, in a small frame building in 1907 or 1908. August Maffey turned one of the three buildings around on the new lot so it faced Blair Street and tore the center one down, leaving the one that Molly Foley and "Denver" Kate lived in located near the rear of the lot. He later added an upstairs to the building, where he housed his family. Julia Maffey

Fig. 21 *Second French Bakery on the southeast corner of 13th and Blair streets. Left to right: Mrs. August Maffey in window, Joe Machetto, Mrs. Pedroni, Julia Maffey holding Pedroni Baby. Others unknown. Joe Machetto operated a mailorder clothing business in front of bakery. Samples of cloth in window. The "Club" sign was a piece of used glass, it was not the name of the store. Julia Maffey Photo.*

and her mother arrived from Tuscany, Italy in 1908. Julia remembered moving to the new store in 1909. It is possible that Maffey and Machetto leased the property prior to buying it in 1910. The building served as the French Bakery until 1916, when the business was moved into the Teller House on Greene Street. Joe Machetto was the baker and August Maffey the salesman. They would make baskets of French Bread each day and deliver them to the boarding houses and bordellos along Blair Street. Later the building was used by "Diamond Tooth" Leona as a crib.

Fig. 22 Barney Tocco's Piemonte Grocery and Shoe Store. Taken about 1950. Now occupied by Ruth Ward's Candle and Gift Shop. Building was originally a crib, built in 1900. Jim Bell Collection.

BARNEY TOCCO'S

In 1916, Barney Tocco and his wife, opened Blair Street's first "convenience and shoe store" in the building now occupied by Ruth Ward's Candle and Gift Shop. He sold basic groceries and supplies, along with shoes, to the women of the "line." Up until 1916, Barney Tocco worked as a miner. He was from Piemonte, Italy.

His store was originally built as a crib about 1900 by C. C. H. Kramer, a local butcher. It passed through several hands in the intervening years. On October 4, 1916, Caterina Giono sold the crib to Barney and his wife. They operated the store together until Barney's death in 1937. Mrs. Tocco continued the store until her death in May 1951. She always added the caption, "In memory of Barney Tocco," to her newspaper ads.

Fig. 23 1954 photo of Barney Tocco's old store (left) and Louis Satore's crib (right). Signs from movie set. Ruth Gregory Collection.

Fig. 24 Barney Tocco's old store, now the Candle and Gift Shop. 1986. Allan Bird Photo.

Fig. 25 Barney Tocco's advertising ruler. Courtesy of Annie Smith. Allan Bird Photo.

Fig. 26 Photo of Barney Tocco 1868-1937, taken from his gravestone. 1987. Allan Bird Photo.

Fig. 27 Original George Boss Livery Stable on the northeast corner of 13th and Blair streets. Later operated by Joe Augustine. Mrs. Augustine kept cows and ran a dairy until after World War II. Sign from movie set. 1954 Photo. Ruth Gregory Collection.

THE LIVERY STABLES

On the northeast corner of 13th and Blair, after the first French Bakery shop was built, George Boss bought four lots from the town of Silverton and built a livery stable. This was taken over by the Joe Augustine family and operated as a livery stable and dairy until after World War II. John Matties remembers helping Mrs. Augustine deliver milk after the war. The stable was clearly visible in the motion picture "Night Passage," filmed in 1957. After the Augustine's left, Mr. Curtis, the local barber, owned the building. Snow collapsed the front portion of the building during the mid-1970's. The back portion still remains. Silverton's 1883 stone county jail is enclosed in the back of the old stable.

Adjacent to Mattivi's Monte Carlo, to the south, was a livery stable operated by the Mattivi family. This stable occupied the site of one of Silverton's oldest bordello's.

The Doud Brothers kept a corral on Blair Street behind their Exchange Livery, on Greene Street. The corral occupied the site of the present White Woman Store and a portion of the Chamber of Commerce "Potty Park."

Fig. 28 1954 photo showing Tomaselli's Boarding House with Zanoni-Pedroni's Saloon at left. Ruth Gregory Collection.

BOARDING HOUSES

Many of the boarding houses on Blair Street were also saloons, and at one time or another, bordellos. These will be discussed in the following chapters. One building, located on the northeast corner of 11th and Blair streets, was used only as a boarding house for miners. It was originally known as the Union House, operated by a Mrs. Mahoney. According to John Matties, it later became the Hood boarding house. Joe Tomaselli purchased the building in May of 1924 and used the building as a private residence and a boarding house for miners until the late 1930's or early 1940's. The building was demolished in the late 1950's and the present Ore Bucket gift shop built on the site.

Several large boarding houses were located on Blair Street between 13th and 14th streets. These buildings are located on the east side of Blair and are utilized today as private residences.

Fig. 28 a. Matilda "Big Tilly" Fattor at left. Joe and Fannie Tomaselli with their children, Anna, Mary, and William. ca. 1910. Mr. & Mrs. Kenneth Jakino Photo.

Jacob Schneider's Residence.

Fig. 29 Jacob Schneider's residence (right) on west side of Blair Street north of 11th Street. This is the oldest Bordello on Blair Street. Was originally occupied by Alice Morris and later by Alice Hanke. Photo taken in 1949 during the filming of the motion picture "Ticket to Tomahawk." Don Stott Photo.

JACOB SCHNEIDER'S CARPENTER SHOP

About the turn of the century, Jacob Schneider purchased Alice Hanke's crib on the west side of Blair Street, just to the north of 11th Street. He turned the old crib into his private residence. He also purchased another crib, a few doors to the north, which he converted into a carpenter shop. This building was built as a crib in 1882 by F. O. Sherwood. His residence was on lot 15 and his shop on lot 17, of block 29. He purchased the two buildings in 1896 and operated until the late 1920's. The building on Lot 17 was torn down in the late 1940's or early 1950's. The original 1877 building now occupies the front half of "Professor Shutterbug's Olde Tyme Photo Studio." The log structure attached to the rear of the building was moved from the ghost town of Middleton during recent times.

The following chapters will describe the various establishments along Blair Street. With the exception of the North Pole Saloon and Boarding House, all were concentrated between 11th and 13th streets.

Fig. 30 Peter Orella's Standard Bottling Works, about 1902, now the Crewl Elephant Gift Shop. Northwest corner of 13th and Blair streets. Orella owned interests in many of Blair Street's bordellos. Jim Bell Collection.

THE STANDARD BOTTLING WORKS

The Standard Bottling Works was owned and operated by Peter Orella. In addition to the bottling works, he owned several of the bordellos on Blair Street. His bottling works occupied the present Crewel Elephant Gift Shop on the northwest corner of 13th and Blair streets.

CHAPTER ELEVEN
THE LAUNDRY

Fig. 31 The Laundry—Original residence built by Jane Bowen in Oct. 1880. Northwest corner of 12th and Blair streets. Sign "Bloom's" was painted for the 1949 movie "Ticket to Tomahawk." Ruth Gregory Collection.

"IF YOU WENT IN WITH ANY MONEY,
YOU CAME OUT CLEAN"
Jim Hook, Sr.

JANE BOWEN

The Laundry occupied Jane Bowen's original 1880 building on the northwest corner of 12th and Blair streets. The building was originally used as a residence and later a dance hall by the Bowens. Much of early day Blair Street history evolved around this building. One of the earliest suicide attempts was made in Jane

Bowen's, in March 1884, by a girl named "Mable." She attempted to take her life with chloroform and failed. The paper mentioned that this was the third time she had attempted the rash act, each time being saved by the town physicians. The fight between "Dutch" Lena and "Irish" Nell took place in this building. The building was also used for town dances or "balls" and such events were usually well attended. During the early years, Jane Bowen ran her dance hall on a seasonal basis, usually closing in November and reopening in late March or early April. She and her husband William, also owned and ran the Westminster Hall Dance Hall and Saloon[19] located directly behind the Blair Street building. They sold Westminster Hall on April 11, 1889, to Charles Jones and Morris Lonergan for $3000. On June 22, 1891, Bill Bowen died of miner's consumption.

After her husband's death, Jane Bowen sold her Blair Street establishment to Joseph Sartore on March 2, 1892, for $1500. She had planned to travel to her home in London. The records show that on August 29, 1892, she purchased the lot on the southeast corner of 12th and Blair streets from George Davis for $350. She built the Palace Dance Hall which was later to become the National Hall. She actually completed the new building during the second week of August, before the newspapers reported her purchase of the land.

LUDWIG'S DANCE HALL

On January 29, 1894, Joseph Sartore sold an undivided half-interest in his new dance hall to Ludwig Vota for $750. Vota took over the management of the property and it became known as Ludwig's Dance Hall. The newspapers once referred to it as "Ludwig's Pest House." In August 1894, the partners decided to renovate the hall and turn it into a variety theater. After a short unsuccessful effort, they soon realized where the money was to be made and quickly turned it back into one of the more notorious bordellos and saloons. The August 15, 1896, *Silverton Standard* printed the following event:

CHAPTER ELEVEN

At 11 o'clock last Wednesday night the sound of a pistol shot aroused citizens living in the vicinity of Ludwig's Dance Hall, which developed the fact that Gene Carney had been shot by Charles Shepherd in a fight. The feud had been brewing for some time. The ball of the 32-calibre entering Carney's leg below the knee cap, just at the upper edge of the tibial bone, and ranging downward and out of the lower part of the calf. Blood poisoning set in and he was taken to Durango to have his leg amputated. He later died.

Note: Shepherd was sentenced to forty months in the state penitentiary.

Evidence that the building was used as a bordello is found in the March 27 and April 3, 1897, *Silverton Standard*. The sad death of one of the inmates was described in detail:

Last night Annie James, one of the unfortunates, who had been working at Ludwig Vota's Dance Hall for about a year, swallowed a two ounce bottle of carbolic acid, from the effects of which she died. The poison taken at about 8 o'clock in the evening. Drs. Pascoe and Prewitt were summoned by some of the girl's companions, and did everything in their power to alleviate the sufferings of the unfortunate woman, who was, however, too far gone at the time of their arrival for medical ministrations to have any effect on and she died at 11 o'clock. It seems that the girl from some cause, attributed to a love affair, had become depressed, therefore the rash step which ended her life. She left a note, evidently written to a lover, which was as follows: 'I can't stand your abuse any longer, good bye, (Signed) Annie.' The remains will be shipped to Leadville where the mother of the deceased resides.

April 3, 1897, *Silverton Standard*:

The obsequities of that poor unfortunate, Annie James, of whose untimely death we gave notice in our last issue, occurred from the Peoples Church (Congregational Church) Tuesday afternoon. The Rev. Jordan officiating. To the little graveyard above town, where all are alike, irrespective of either high or low degree, find one common resting place. The remains were followed by friends of the deceased, who, perhaps, felt her loss as companion and friend, fully as keenly as if her life had been passed under more favorable circumstances. We learn that Annie was highly thought of among the sporting class to which she belonged.

THE LAUNDRY

Ludwig Vota's Dance Hall had assumed the reputation of being a rough place. Fights were frequent and often violent. The June 25, 1898, _Silverton Standard_ described what one might encounter on an average night at Ludwig's:

> George Saxton, of Ludwig Vota's Dance Hall was snaked up before F. O'Driscoll's police justice court on the charge of breach of the peace, by night watchman Martin Tighe, Monday morning. The prisoner pleaded guilty to the charge of having beaten a man who had 'insulted' his girl and had also slapped her face and pulled her hair. According to the evidence elicited, the victim of the beating, who is a working man, was down from the mines, enjoying a holiday and dropped into Vota's to dance, got boisterous and perpetrated the offense above mentioned. A quarrel ensued between the champion of the lady's(?) honor and subsequently the affair was supposed to have been settled in Jack Matties' Dance Hall across the way, where, by the by, it seems that Ludwig's man followed the miner, who was quite well 'loaded.' Somewhere, about 3 o'clock in the morning, however, a fight took place on the street in front of Ludwig's pest house between Saxton and the miner. Saxton's witnesses—there being no others in the case—testified that it was a fair fight and that no weapons were used save fists. Saxton was fined $7 and costs, which amounted to $15 which he promptly paid and departed. At about half past three o'clock on the morning in question, Night Watchman Tighe found the miner above mentioned in a helpless condition on the corner of Mineral and 12th streets. He was saturated with blood from head to foot and blood was running from his ears. A deep wound had been inflicted on his forehead which extended to the bone. He was brought uptown, washed, and then conveyed to a hotel, where a physician was summoned to close up the wound by four stitches. The man was too badly injured to appear in court and there's no likelihood of his doing so when he recovers.

"BILLY" LUKE'S

On May 26, 1900, Ludwig Vota leased his interest in Tom Cain's old dance hall to Frank Alphine. Vota also owned several small cribs on Blair Street. Alphine, also spelled Alpine, opened his own dance hall in Tom Cain's old building. About the same time, Sartore and Vota leased their property to William (Billy) Luke to continue as a dance hall. The reputation of being a place that could be dangerous to your health continued.

CHAPTER ELEVEN

The July 7, 1900, *Silverton Standard* reported the following melee:

> Thursday evening a man by the name of James Keegan, who was under the influence of liquor began shooting at Frank Miller in Luke's Dance Hall. Deputy Sheriff Morris, who was standing outside of the place at the time ran into the hall when Keegan turned his attention to the deputy and, Sam Morris, acting on the defense, shot three times at the crazed man. After the smoke had cleared away it was found that Sam was wounded—a bullet having scratched a finger in his left hand. Eight shots were exchanged. The man was arrested and placed in the county jail to await the arrival of District Attorney Spickland.

The following week James Keegan was brought before Justice Watson and fined $25 and costs, amounting to $50 for his fun in target practice. He paid the fine and left the court room rejoicing.

The paper referred to the incident as having happened in Jennie Burwell's Dance Hall. It is assumed the place was known by both names.

"Billy" Luke operated the dance hall for over twenty-five years. On February 20, 1926, Angelina Sartore and Mary Vota, heirs of Joseph Sartore and Ludwig Vota, sold the dance hall to a group of men which included John (Jack) Gilheany, Tom Gilheany, Charlie Longstrom, Tom Olson, and Sam Manuck for $2000. Jack Gilheany and Charlie Longstom operated the property as the "Laundry" between 1926 and 1928 when Gilheany bought out Longstrom. Gilheany continued alone until the early 1940's when he moved to Greene Street.

Fig. 32 Gambling table in the Laundry ca. 1927. Charlie Longstrom (right), Jack Gilheaney's partner, dealing the cards. Carl Longstrom Photo.

HEALTH CONDITIONS IN "BILLY" LUKE'S

The health conditions at the vaious bordellos left much to be desired. Billy Luke's Dance Hall was cited by the Colorado Department of Health as a public health menace. Death of the inmates from both suicide and disease was not uncommon. Pneumonia was a killer disease in the early days of Silverton and many of the girls passed from this earth as a result of this dread malady.

February 2, and May 25, 1901, the *Silverton Standard* printed the obituary of two of these girls:

On February 2, 1901, at 3 o'clock Wednesday morning, from a life that was black to the blind, 'Madge,' one of the girls employed at Luke's Dance Hall, crossed the channel of death into the vale of mystery. The disease was pneumonia and the burial occurred from Prosser's undertaking establishment at 3 o'clock Thursday afternoon.

On May 25, 1901, Ella Keeton, a poor unfortunate who operated at Luke's Dance Hall for the past six weeks, died on Wednesday morning at about 11 o'clock. The woman was about forty years old and the disease which removed her from the glitter of dance hall life, was pneumonia. A subscription was raised among the sporting fraternity sufficient to defray the expense of burial. Rev. George Eaves made a good talk at the funeral which occurred from Prosser's Undertaking Room Thursday afternoon at 2 o'clock.

Dancing might be listed among the many hazards of the early dance halls. In April of 1904, R. K. Reed, a local photographer sustained a serious fracture of the right leg above the ankle in a fall while dancing at Luke's Dance Hall. The girl that he was dancing with was a waitress at the Grand (Grand Imperial) Hotel and because of the accident, her presence was observed by the law. She was informed that if she were to dance in a dance hall she would have to purchase the usual license. The following week the paper reported that "the Grand Hotel is a waitress short these strenuous times."

CHAPTER ELEVEN

JACK GILHEANY'S "LAUNDRY"

The late Eddie Lorenzon remembered Jack Gilheany's "Laundry" as, "having a restaurant in front, a dance floor in the center and gambling rooms in the rear with the girls upstairs. This was early, possibly before Jack Gilheany." The late Jim Hook, Sr., remembered the Laundry as, "having an attractive decor with fresh paint, wallpaper, and tin ceilings. It was warmed by a large pot-bellied stove in the corner." He believed that the gambling rooms were in the center and the girls in the back rooms. A dance floor was also available adjacent to the gambling area. Mary Swanson recalls that there was a restaurant called the "Broken Elbow" in the front of the building. Several "old timers" recalled that the girls were upstairs and the gambling was in the back of the building during Gilheany's management.

Gilheany had the reputation of being too kind for his own good. He was best remembered for his aid to the wives of the compulsive gamblers who consistently gambled away their entire paychecks when they had families to feed. Corky Scheer recalls that a Frank Sierra, "who had the fever bad," would lose his entire check. Jack Gilheany would take half of what Frank lost and deliver it to his wife and kids so they could buy groceries.

One lady commented: "When her husband lost his entire paycheck at Gilheany's nothing was ever returned to her."

In the early 1940's, Gilheany moved from the Laundry building to the Club Saloon on Greene Street, which was located a few doors to the north of the Grand Imperial Hotel. The exact time of his move is not known. He sold the "Laundry" building to Annie Smith on February 18, 1948. She bought the structure for salvage and tore down the rear portion of the building in 1952 and the remainding original 1880 building in 1957 or 1958. Gilheany died in 1956.

Fig. 33 *High Noon Hamburger Stand—1986, former site of the Laundry. Allan Bird Photo.*

The present High Noon Hamburger Stand occupies the site of one of Silverton's largest bordellos.

---

[19] Westminster Hall was on the northeast corner of 12th and Greene streets, where the brick Benson Building now stands.

Presently Natalia's 1912 Restaurant

Fig. 34 Late 1883 photo showing original Nell Castell House, later to become the Matties'
Boarding House. Now occupied by an antique shop. Colo. Hist. Soc. Photo.

The Matties Boarding House is the oldest bordello still standing and is located on the west side of Blair Street south of 12th. The building is now occupied by an antique shop and Natalia's 1912 Restaurant. The original building was constructed in 1883 by John Curry, the owner of the *La Plata Miner* newspaper. The present structure is a composite of two buildings. The later building, which contained the Welcome Saloon (now Natalia's), was added in 1909. The old frame building was built on a plan similar to Jane Bowen's Dance Hall. It's possible that the same contractor built both buildings.

NELL CASTELL

On July 16, 1887, John Curry sold the building to Nell Castell, one of the early day Madames of Blair Street, for $1400. It's possible that she had been renting the building since its construction. It was not uncommon for a woman to lease a building, operate for a few years and then purchase the property. Nell was first mentioned in the December 5, 1885, *La Plata Miner* in connection with the knifing of the proprietor of the Hub Saloon which was located on the south side of13th Street west of Greene Street. The article read:

> The tracks of blood leading from the Hub Saloon along Thirteenth Street were the subject of much comment on Monday morning, and from the quantity of blood spilled it really seemed as though some one had bled to death. Subsequent inquiry elicited the facts that Frank Cooper, the proprietor of the Hub, had been cut in the hand while in the act of defending himself from an enraged woman, who sprang at him with a clasp knife. Frank caught the knife, and as the blade was drawn through, it left an ugly gash in the palm of his hand. The difficulty had begun in the Fashion when it is said that Frank refused to dance with the woman, Nell Castell, and she then followed him to the saloon with the results stated.

The following year, 1888, the building was assessed to the estate of Deliah Curry, John Curry's late wife. This would indicate that Nell Castell was not able to complete the payments on the property. Sometime between 1888 and 1894 ownership of the house passed from the Deliah Curry estate to Mr. E. L. Roberts, a local hardware owner and real estate investor. The building made news in the May 19, 1894, *Silverton Standard*, which reported a near fatal break-in:

> Friday night, the 11 last, the old Nellie Castell House on Blair Street, now standing vacant and owned by E. L. Roberts, was broken into and a few articles of every day crockeryware were packed off. The following night, Roberts, armed with a 6-shooter, stayed in the house. Somewhat before daybreak Sunday morning, his nibbs, the burglar, returned after another invoice of plunder, and while engaged in the dark of tapping a closet of wash bowls, etc. Mr. Roberts 'drew bead' and fired—the bullet however, happily for the burglar missing its mark—the nocturnal depredator making good his escape through the back door.

LOUISA CRAWFORD

That same year, on September 28, 1894, E. L. Roberts sold the lot and building to Jack Matties. Matties borrowed $700 of the purchase price as a first mortgage from Roberts. On September 3, 1895, Matties paid off the note and received a quit-claim deed to the property. Two months later, Roberts sold the vacant lot to the north of the building to Louisa Crawford. In 1896, a year later, both properties were assessed to Louisa Crawford. The lot directly south of the original bordello, was assessed to both Crawford and Matties. Louisa Crawford operated the large building as a dance hall and on March 23, 1897, a fight requiring the services of a physician, occurred in "Louisa's Dance Hall." The paper reported that the fight was between two Italians. The following week, Joseph Sartore from Piemonte Province, Italy, was quick to point out that the fight was between two Austrians from the Tyrol and not Italians. Mr. Sartore stated that "the Italians are peaceable and seldom fight." This is one of the earliest references to the Tyrolean-Piemonte feud.

Louisa Crawford and Jack Matties were married in 1897. They sold the dance hall to Jennie Walker, another lady of the night. She had possession of the building for only a few months when she defaulted on her mortgage and the property was returned to Louisa Crawford Matties. Jack Matties took over the operation of the dance hall.

On January 6, 1898, the _Silverton Standard_ reported a rip-roaring fight which occurred at "Louisa's":

Jealousy, through unrequited love, worked up to a fever heat, by copious libations of bad whiskey, was the cause of the row that occurred, Thursday night at the dance hall formerly occupied by Louisa. Both thumping and pistol shots were indulged in; the piano player of the concern, at a very early stage of the game, having discharged his little 'pop' three times in rapid succession at the frontispiece of a gentleman from Mexico, who however, didn't get hit worth a cent, and, along with three companions also from Mexico mounted the marksman and hammered the life nearly out of him. The night watch, who was walking past the dance hall at the time of the fracas, heard a cry for help and upon entering the bar room, found the musician on the floor with the tropical gentlemen on top of him, beating the devil's tattoo on his head and ribs, while the frail, fair ones of the house stood around in an attitude of prayer.

All the participants of the row were pulled, and yesterday were brought before Justice of the Peace Watson. From the testimony of the witnesses, it appears that a woman, who of late has been before the dread tribunal of justice quite frequently, and also, a Mexican woman, were the modern Delilahs, who brought their Sampsons to grief by capping up the row. Nearly all the witnesses were women of the avenue, only two or three having testified. The judge was very lenient and with the milk of human kindness oozing from his Websterian brow, he imposed fines on the discordant ones, of from five to ten dollars and costs, each.

In an effort to expand his saloon and dance hall business on Blair Street, Jack and Louisa Matties expanded their enterprise. Jack built a small frame lean-to 25 X 35 feet in size onto the north side of the dance hall and opened the Welcome Saloon. Jack leased Jane Bowen's Dance Hall.[20] They operated Bowen's old hall and their Welcome Saloon and Dance Hall.

JACK MATTIES

Jack Matties was the uncle of John and Joe Matties, both now deceased. John was born in 1909 and Joe a few years later. Both gentlemen resided in Denver and when interviewed about their uncle Jack remembered their parents saying that he had a rather violent temper and he liked to flash his wealth. He would often carry large sums of cash on his person. In the spring of 1898, the *Silverton Standard* reported the following story about how Jack narrowly escaped death on the road to Ouray, the present day Million Dollar Highway:

Jack Matties, while enroute to Silverton from Ouray, narrowly escaped death. While riding a Ouray livery horse, this side of the toll gate, the animal became frightened and Jack just dismounted in time to see the horse go over the trail to the creek, 500 feet below.

According to John and Joe Matties, the real story was quite different from that printed in the paper. It seems the horse refused to go and Jack became so infuriated, he pushed the horse over the cliff.

During the summer of 1903, Jack Matties decided to visit his home in Trento, Tyrol, Austria. When he left America he was carrying between $5000 and $6000 in gold coin on his person, this was about twenty pounds of gold. He left Silverton on July 25, and was never heard from again. In November of 1903, his body was discovered in a river in present day Monaco. He was murdered and robbed in a railroad passenger compartment, and thrown from the train. He left real estate valued at $5000 in Silverton. After his death, his mother who lived in Tressila-Pina, Civezzana, Tyrol, Austria, quit-claimed her interest in the Silverton saloon to Battiste, Jack's brother. It is not known how she obtained an interest in the property. Her name was Mattivi. Jack's real name was Giacomo Mattivi. He changed his name to Matties because there were several other Mattivis in Silverton and the postmaster kept getting their mail mixed up.

When his brother Battiste heard of his death, he immediately left for Europe to recover his brother's body and attempt to track down his murderers. The culprits were never apprehended. Battiste returned to Silverton to operate his saloon and dance hall.

Jack's widow, Louisa Crawford Matties, cleared out the tenants from the dance hall and lived there alone, giving the Welcome Saloon to her brother-in-law Battiste.

BATTISTE MATTIES

Battiste Matties was born in Tyrol, Austria. His first wife died during childbirth in 1894. The child, who was named Maria, was delivered by instruments and was crippled in the process of birth. Battiste, unable to care for the child himself, placed the baby girl in a convent. Despondent after his wife's death, Battiste decided to come to America and join his brother Jack. Jack sent him the money to cover the expense of the trip.

MATTIE'S BOARDING HOUSE & WELCOME SALOON

On July 1, 1901, Jack Matties sold his dance hall to his brother Battiste, John and Joe's father. He charged Battiste $6000 for the building. This was the highest price ever received for a Blair Street dance hall.

In September 1905, Battiste decided to return to Austria and find a wife. During his absence he leased his dance hall and saloon to Peter Ferari and Gio Corrazzo. Peter Ferari was the attorney for Battiste Matties and was probably leasing the property as an investment. Gio Corrazzo operated the Welcome Saloon and Dance Hall.

In 1906, while visiting his home in Trento, Tyrol, Austria, Battiste visited a small inn. While there he became enamored with a young woman working for the inn. He proposed marriage and she accepted. She was seventeen years old, just shy of being eighteen. He was thirty eight. When Battiste and his young bride returned to Silverton, Louisa Matties moved to Chicago, leaving the property to the newlyweds. After a few years, she broke off contact with the family and was never heard from again.

Battiste's bride's name was Anne Ottilia; however, she went by the name of Ottilia. He brought her back to America and converted the dance hall into a boarding house for miners. By the time she was twenty-three, she had four children. In addition to her own family, she insisted in bringing Battiste's daughter Maria from the convent in Austria.

Fig. 35 Matties' Boarding House (left) built in 1882, and Welcome Saloon (right) built in 1909. Note old roof line (arrow) of original Nell Castell House. Jim Bell Collection.

In 1909, Battiste tore down the old lean-to saloon and replaced it with a large addition, having a saloon downstairs and twelve rooms upstairs. He added a lean-to kitchen onto the original building. The saloon was equipped with a 22-foot-long back bar with mirror, a regulation-size bowling alley, a player piano and slot machines. He installed the attractive iron front that graces the front of the building today. For years Ottilia ran the boarding house, charging $1 a day for room and board, which included laundry, room cleaning and packed lunches for the miners.

Fig. 36 1954 photo showing Matties boarding house and old Welcome Saloon. Note change of windows. Ruth Gregory Collection.

They heated the building with coal. Each room had a small stove. This was done to eliminate bed bugs. The buildings, such as the Benson Hotel, that used steam heat were crawling with bed bugs. For some reason the bugs liked high humidity. The basement of the boarding house would hold a railroad car of coal. Often during the bitter cold months when the railroad would be closed for extended periods because of snow slides blocking the track, the Mattieses would keep much of the town supplied with coal.

During the flu epidemic of 1918, John and Joe reported that the majority of the women on Blair Street acted as nurses. Silverton had the highest per capita death rate of any town in the nation. Over 148 people died in about three weeks. Many of the women of the "line" who acted as nurses were exposed to the deadly flu and many paid with their lives. A woman of the "line," by the name of Bessie Miller, who was the sister of "Sheeny" Pearl, contracted

the majority of the women on Blair Street acted as nurses during the flu epidemic of 1918

the deadly disease. Battiste took her in and put her in the front room of the boarding house. The next morning he found her dead in her room. She was one of the first victims of the epidemic. Mr. Matties made an infirmary of his house and fed the sick homemade chicken broth mixed with red wine. Only one of his patients died. He made large kettles of this broth for all of the hospitals and make-shift infirmaries in town. Otillia and her two sons, John and William were deathly ill with the flu. They all survived.

Fig. 37 Matties' Boarding House and Welcome Saloon—1990. Now Antique Shop (left) and Natalia's 1912 Restaurant (right). Allan Bird Photo.

The Matties family was raised in the boarding house. As small boys, about 1920, John and Joe would earn much of their spending money by running errands for the prostitutes on Blair Street. This was the main source of income for many of the young people in Silverton. They would walk up and down the street and watch the doors. If the door was closed and the red light was off, this meant that the girl had a customer. If the women needed groceries or other supplies from Greene Street, they would leave their doors ajar and beckon to the boys with their finger. They

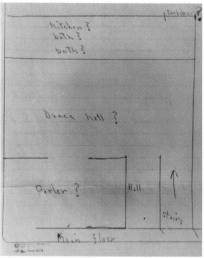

Fig. 38 Approximate floor plan of Jack Matties' (Old Nell Castell House) Dance Hall before 1903. John Matties sketch.

would make a list, enclose the money and list in an envelope, and the boys would deliver the supplies to them. They would receive twenty-five cents for the errand. This was a fortune in 1920. It was the acceptable way to earn money as long as the boys were small. When they reached high school age, they were cursed at by the women and told to "get the hell out of here, you little S.O.B.'s." It

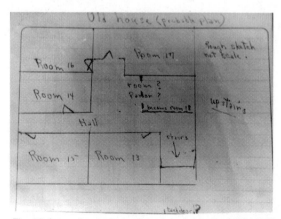

Fig. 39 Approximate floor plan of Jack Matties' (Old Nell Castell House). Bordello upstairs above the dance hall. John Matties sketch.

was understood by the women that they were never to solicit on the streets and this rule was rigidly enforced. In later years, during the late 1920's and 1930's, the women were allowed to visit Greene Street to pick up their mail, do their shopping and have dinner between the hours of four and six in the afternoon. The

MATTIE'S BOARDING HOUSE & WELCOME SALOON

American Cafe, which was located in the present lobby of the Grand Imperial Hotel, was the favorite eating place of the Blair Street women. The "girls" would be seated at a table and a curtain pulled around them to shield the "good" people of Silverton from their presence. Bill Moute ran the American Cafe. He was the "special" friend of "21" Pearl Thompson, owner of the Mikado.

On March 8, 1924, Battiste deeded the property to his wife Ottilia and her three sons, John, Joe, and William. Less than a month later, on April 2, 1924, Battiste Matties died.

Fig. 40 1936 photo of the Matties Boarding House and Welcome Saloon. William Matties (deceased) in doorway. John and Joe Matties photo.

The building remained in the Matties family until 1947, when they sold it for $5500. The boarding house is now occupied by an antique shop and the Welcome Saloon is now Natalia's 1912 Restaurant. The old wooden frame of the building has been altered and stucco has been applied to the outer walls of the old boarding house.

---

[20] This was Jane Bowen's Palace Dance Hall on the southeast corner of 12th and Blair streets, later to become the National Hall.

CHAPTER TWELVE

Fig. 41 Several members of the Matties family in front of their Welcome Saloon with guests from Rock Springs, Wyoming. Maria Matties is in front center with long dress. Joe Matties is at front left. Late 1930 photo. John and Joe Matties Photo.

Fig. 42 Battiste Matties about 1910. John and Joe Matties Photo.

Fig. 43 Joe Matties (left) and John Matties (right). May, 1986. Both now deceased. Allan Bird Photo.

CHAPTER THIRTEEN
JOHN WEBB
"FATTY" COLLINS' PLACE

Fig. 44 John Webb "Fatty" Collins' Saloon and Bordello. Built in late 1883. The Alhambra Theater is next door to the south. Looking east toward the river. Denver Public Library West. Hist. Dept.

Little is known about the Collins house. It was built in 1883, about the same time as the Matties house and the Alhambra Theater, which was next door to the south. The house was rather large, using the same architecture as Jane Bowen's and the Matties' boarding house. "Fatty" Collins was a Silverton saloon man. The Collins house was never mentioned in the local newspapers; therefore, we can only assume its function. It was probably a bordello with a saloon for the customers.[21] "Fatty" Collins died sometime between 1884 and 1887. The building probably remained vacant after his death. On August 23, 1890, the local paper announced that: "Mrs. Harris purchased the building next to the

Alhambra and will move it on to Main Street." Until this time, the building was assessed at $800, which suggested a rather large structure.

F. F. Martin bought the lot from the Collins estate In 1901 for $100. He built a three-girl crib across the entire twenty-five-foot frontage of the lot. About this time the city of Silverton instigated a street numbering system which must have been influenced by the small cribs which lined Blair Street. The numbers started at two on the east side of the street and ran to 72 toward the north. On the west side of the street the numbers ran from one to 71. A new number was assigned for every 8 1/3 feet of the block. Thus Martin's new three-girl crib had three addresses, one for each crib. The farthest crib to the south was 1154 Blair, the center crib 1156, and the northernmost crib 1158.

Molly Foley lived at 1158 for a short time. Other occupants were Dorothy Reon and Tempis Burke, who occupied the first crib at 1154 Blair. Irene Gilbert lived in the center crib. The information about the street addresses of the various women was obtained from notes left by Louis Dalla. Before his death, Dalla had planned to write a history of Silverton and had listed the names and addresses of most of the businesses and "interesting" people in Silverton.

In the early 1920's, the building was moved to the back of the lot and used as a residence. The area adjacent to the street, where the building once stood, was converted into a garden. The building was later demolished and the lot has remained vacant until the present time.

21 The building was located on the east side of Blair Street, just south of 12th on the lot directly north of the "Green House."

CHAPTER FOURTEEN
THE
"GREEN HOUSE"

Fig. 45 Early view of the Alhambra Theater and "Fatty" Collin's place, looking west toward Greene Street. Theater existed from late 1883 to 1891, when it was destroyed by fire. Colo. Hist. Soc. Photo.

FORMER SITE OF THE ALHAMBRA THEATER

The old Alhambra Theater was built by William Snyder in late 1883 and leased by two gentlemen by the names of J. E. Jones and Fred Barry. The first mention of the Alhambra was in the December 4, 1884, San Juan Herald: "The residence of one of the actresses at the Alhambra, No. 444 Blair Street, was broken into and $140 cash was taken. No clue to the thief."

The address, 444 Blair Street, cannot be located using the new (1901) numbering system. No buildings ever existed in what would be the 400 block of Blair Street today.

115

Fig. 46 Mid-1880's view of east side of Greene Street, between 12th and 13th streets, showing the Fashion Theater and Gambling Hall, Goode's Saloon, and the Exchange Livery. All buildings on the block have been replaced. Andy Hanahan Photo.

The Alhambra was originally a saloon, dance hall, gambling establishment, and variety theater. In the mid-1880's, Silverton had two variety theaters, the Alhambra and the Temple of Fashion, commonly referred to as the Fashion. The September 5, 1885, *Silverton Democrat-Herald* printed the following: "Silverton continues to support two variety shows, and both report an increasing volume of business."

Fig. 47 1883 sketch of the interior of the Fashion Gambling Hall and Variety Theater. Greene Street, Silverton. From the Nov. 23, 1883, Silverton Democrat.

THE "GREEN HOUSE"

The Alhambra was located on the west side of Blair Street just south of 12th Street.[22] In 1884, the Alhambra was assessed $800, the same as its neighbor to the north, "Fatty" Collins. The fact that it also served as a gambling house is confirmed by a September 26, 1885, comment in the *La Plata Miner* which read: "Two Swedes blew in their pile at the Alhambra the other evening, said to amount to $200."

In September 1885, shortly before the November local elections, Sheriff William Sullivan was running for reelection. His undersheriff, Harry LeRoy, bet him any amount that he would not be reelected. This, of course, did not sit well with Sullivan. A general bit of hard feelings developed in the Alhambra, while they "were taking in the sights." (*La Plata Miner*) During the row Sullivan slapped LeRoy and made allusions "to his immediate ancestors." LeRoy failed to fight back. Later in the Metropolitan Saloon, on Greene Street, the two men came to blows. Sullivan felt a pistol in LeRoy's coat and proceeded to grab it and throw it away. The crowd was anticipating a good fist fight, but LeRoy, it is reported, "staggered against the bar, and cried like a baby."

In October of 1885, the operators of the Alhambra, Jones and Barry, dissolved their partnership with Jones, taking over the business.

In June 1886, the previously related story of the fight between ladies of easy virtue, "Oregon Short Line" vs. "Irish" Nell, "Dutch" Lena and Minnie, "the baby Jumbo," occurred in the inner sanctums of the Alhambra.

The theater portion of the enterprise was seasonal, usually opening about the end of June and closing in late October or early November. Many of the best variety shows of the times were booked at the Alhambra theater.

It is not known how profitable the variety theater business was in early Silverton but the ownership of the Alhambra changed frequently. The following "for sale" notice was published in the

CHAPTER FOURTEEN

August 7, 1886, *Silverton Democrat*:

> "The Alhambra, one of the best-paying variety theaters in Colorado is offered for sale by the proprietor who is compelled to leave the country on account of ill health."

An example of the type of entertainment provided at the Alhambra was given in the October 9, 1886, *Silverton Democrat*:

> The Alhambra Theater is growing in popularity nightly. The program offered is one so varied that the taste of all is satisfied except the vulgar minded. The trapeze performance of Mr. and Mrs. Bickets is a marvel in its way, and the difficult and thrilling feats nightly performed by them is hailed with shouts of delight. The vaudeville performance of Miss Hall and Bob Thies is quite original in conception—especially so is that of Bob's wonderful leg contortions. The King Children are immense in their songs, dances, etc. Maggie LeClair has established herself as the standing favorite by her neat wardrobe and good acting, while Clarry and Behan can not be excelled in their line. To the Jones Brothers, proprietors and Jimmie Griffith, stage manager, is due the entire success of the theater, who seek to give the public none but first class artists.

The trapeze artist, Minnie Bicket missed the rope about a week after the above review was published. She fell fifteen feet and lost two teeth plus suffering numerous bruises.

Silverton had a man by the name of J. W. Cory, who was an attorney of sorts. He had a rather violent temper and was frequently being put in jail for shooting at someone. He often defended the prostitutes of Blair Street and spent most of his time in saloons, drinking. In 1885, while acting as attorney for a girl who claimed she had been raped, Cory ended up in jail for attempting to rape her. On the night of July 8, 1887, the *Silverton Democrat* published the following excerpt on J. W. Cory:

> J. W. Cory is again in trouble—Last night he got into a fight at the Alhambra and got the worst of the encounter. He went off and got a gun and on his return shot into the crowd, but as he did not have a "scatter" gun, he did not succeed in winging any of the gang. He was arrested and lodged in jail. He will have a preliminary hearing this afternoon before Judge O'Driscoll.

THE "GREEN HOUSE"

Cory made the papers again shortly after New Years day. He made a resolution to swear off Demon Delight for the rest of his life. He was applauded by the paper and encouraged to continue on his noble experiment. Unfortunately, it wasn't long before he was shooting at someone again. Fortunately, he was a poor shot.

Prize fights were a frequent event at the Alhambra. The Alhambra would book professional fighters to come to Silverton and put on a "fight to the finish." In November of 1887, two fighters, Johnson and Slatterly, were scheduled to perform at the Alhambra. Neither man had ever been whipped in the ring. Shortly before the scheduled fight, Slatterly, who was from Leadville, got rather obnoxious one evening in the Metropolitan Saloon. Ex-mayor F. M. Snowden, one of Silverton's earliest pioneers, attempted to quiet the man down and was threatened by the belligerent pugilist. Snowden decked him in "two rounds." The following morning Slatterly was arrested, after having his head stitched up. The scheduled fight at the Alhambra continued as planned. After twenty-one rounds, neither man could knock out the other. The fight was declared a draw.

In 1888, William Snyder, the owner of the property, sold the Alhambra to James W. Jones, his renter. Fred Barry and Ed Clarry took over management of the operation for Jones until July 5, 1890, when Cretcher and Shields took over as managers for Jones. They made a basic mistake in advertising and changed the name from the Alhambra to the Red Light. Few of the good people of Silverton would attend a theater named the "Red Light." The name was appropriate for the location, but the net result was poor cash flow. By the end of August, the name was changed back to the Alhambra.

In 1890, the Alhambra was in financial trouble. The September 13, 1890, _Silverton Standard_ reported: "Three new people will be at the Alhambra Monday night and a week from Monday four new ones will arrive. The house is giving a very fine entertainment and deserves a more liberal patronage that it is receiving".

A few weeks later, the building was sold to Mr. John Estep, who took full charge of the operation. Estep got off to a rather rough start with his first booking. He hired a singer and after the performance, Estep presented the "artist" with brick ham. In his presentation speech, Estep reminded the singer that "the ham was not so much in appreciation of his singing as of his gall."

The Alhambra closed for the winter in the fall of 1890, and was preparing to open in early June when fire struck. On May 27, 1891, between four and five o'clock in the morning, black clouds of smoke were seen in the vicinity of 12th and Blair Streets. The firemen made a valiant attempt to save the structure, but could do nothing but save the nearby buildings. Two men were asleep upstairs at the time of the fire and were awakened by the smoke. When they tried to escape, the stairs were engulfed in flames and they were forced to jump from the second story windows to the wooden sidewalk below. Both were slightly injured but soon recovered. One man left his wallet with sixty dollars in crisp bills enclosed. A few days later, while sifting through the ashes, the wallet was recovered, thoroughly charred on the outside but inside, the crisp bills remained unharmed. The cause of the fire was definitely arson and no one seemed to have the slightest idea who could have caused this calamity. It may have been coincidental but the same issue of the *Silverton Standard* that reported on the fire also ran the following short article:

> George Davis and A. W. Dane have taken a lease for eighteen months on the building next to Col. Breens store (next door to present Pickle Barrel Restaurant) and will fix it up for dances and theatrical companies. They will put in a new floor and repaper and paint the building. A stage 25 X 22 feet will be erected at the rear end and the roof of the building over the stage will be raised ten feet. The hall will be a great accommodation as at the present time there is no suitable building in town for traveling companies.

It does make one wonder, doesn't it? After the fire, the lot remained vacant until 1897, when the present "Green House" was built. The building was designed as a four-girl crib with two cribs on the ground floor and two upstairs. The front part of the present building looks very much as it did when it was built, except for the balcony and porch, which were added in the late 1950's. The rear portion of the present building was added in the 1950's or 1960's to accommodate the tourist trade.

THE "GREEN HOUSE"

Fig. 48 The "Green House", east side of Blair Street south of 12th Street. Originally a four-girl crib. Upper door was for shaking rugs—1897 to present. Built on site of the Alhambra Theater. Photo taken about 1949. Jim Bell Collection.

The first units of the four-unit building were sold much like condominiums are today. On June 12, 1897, Fred Barry sold an undivided 1/4 interest in the land and building to Minnie Haugh for $100. She purchased her own crib. In October of 1900, Fred Barry and W. D. Watson gave a quit-claim deed for their interest in the property to John N. Kloster for $200. Kloster and his wife were Silverton business people who invested in Blair Street properties for their rental value. In 1901, Minnie Sanborn, another soiled dove, purchased one of the units for $35. This tells something of the shabby and cheap construction of cribs. In 1905, Kloster's sold the property to James Friel and Ethel Leland for $500. James Friel borrowed $500 from Ludwig Vota for nine months, using the property as collateral. He failed to repay the loan and the property reverted to Vota.

Vota continued to lease the cribs to various women over the years. Pearl Silas, Kate Starr, Mayme Murphy and later, "Jew"

Fanny lived and worked in this bordello. The property remained in the Vota family until September 15, 1937. The building passed through several hands during the following years. Today the building is occupied by the Shady Lady Saloon and Restaurant and a small gift shop. The rear portion of the building and porch have been added in recent times. No one knows when the house ceased to be used as a working crib. Probably in the late 1930's. For some unknown reason, the house has always been painted green.

Fig. 49 Tourist-staged Blair Street gun fight, about 1955. "Green House" is in the center of the photo. Tom Savich Photo.

Fig. 50 "Green House" in 1992. Allan Bird Photo.

22   On the site of the "Green" House, just to the south of where the train stops.

CHAPTER FIFTEEN
ZANONI-PEDRONI'S
FLORENCE SALOON AND BOARDING HOUSE
Presently Bent Elbow Restaurant

Fig. 51 The Zanoni-Pedroni Florence Saloon and Boarding House. Taken about 1939. Present Bent Elbow Restaurant. Jim Bell Collection.

The site of the present Bent Elbow Restaurant was the location of one of Silverton's oldest large buildings, probably one of the early bordellos. Absolutely nothing was ever written in the local newspapers about this structure. The building was built in 1883 by F. O. Sherwood, about the same time as Matties', "Fatty" Collins', and the Alhambra. Sherwood was a local contractor. It is visible in early photos of Blair Street. Judging from the tax

123

assessment, which was $2000 in 1883, the structure was about twice the size of the above buildings. The building may have covered two lots, which would account for the high assessment. Since there were about one hundred and thirty prostitutes working in Silverton during this period of time, it is probable that this was one of the larger "houses."

By 1887, the ownership was transferred to George H. Roberts. The assessment had dropped to $1200. In 1888, Roberts sold the property to Mrs. Emma T. Harris, the same woman that bought "Fatty" Collins' building. The assessment continued to drop to $1000. Historically, there is a ten month break in Silverton newspapers in 1889. Suddenly, the tax assessment on Lots 10 and 11, Block 30 was $0. We can only assume that the building burned in 1889.

The lot remained in the Harris family until 1906 when the estate of W. D. Harris, Emma Harris' husband, sold the lot to Ernest Zanoni. On May 3, 1907, F. O. Sherwood, the previous owner in 1884, issued a warranty deed to Ernest Zanoni for $500. Zanoni had recently arrived in America from Tuscany, Italy. On July 5, 1907, Ernest Zanoni sold half-interest in the land to Louis Pedroni, also from Tuscany. Zanoni and Pedroni used the land and a promise to mortgage "all buildings and fixtures which may hereafter be placed or erected on the foundations now standing on said premises" as collateral for a $2500 loan from Mrs. Thomas Annear. Tom Annear was a successful Silverton businessman who later served on the Colorado Legislature in Denver. Construction began in the fall of 1907 or the early spring of 1908. No buildings were assessed on this lot in 1907. Often if buildings were not completed until the last few month of the year, they were not assessed until the following year. They named their new building the Florence Saloon after their home town in Italy. The Florence Saloon was never a bordello. The first floor was a saloon and the upstairs served as a residence and boarding house for miners.

On February 11, 1909, Louis Pedroni issued a warranty deed to Ernest Zanoni for his half-interest in the property. On October

14, 1913, four years later, Zanoni let Pedroni buy back his original half-interest in the business. In 1914, the Zanoni and Pedroni families mortgaged the property to Peter Orella, owner of the Standard Bottling Works (Present Crewel Elephant building) for $4326.79. Two years later the debt was repaid. Orella issued a warranty deed to Guisipina Zanoni for $1000. It was now 1917, and Pedroni had never paid Zanoni for his 1913 sale. Zanoni brought suit against Pedroni in his native land of Florence, Italy. The lawyers for both parties got their heads together and decided that both men were wealthy. They delayed settlement of the suit for four years, all the time collecting their inflated fees. Finally the court ruled in favor of Zanoni; however, by the time the Attorney's fees had been paid, Zanoni had little, if any, gain.

Fig. 52 The Zanoni-Pedroni Florence Bar ca. 1912. Andy Hanahan Photo.

Ernest Zanoni was also a miner. He obtained leases on several excellent mining properties, including the Silver Lake Mine. He had twenty men working for him in 1918. He also leased the Golden Fleece Mine which contained a narrow, but rich vein of metallic gold. In 1921, Ernest Zanoni retired to his native Italy with a stake of about $250,000.

Descendants of the Zanoni family still live in Durango and Silverton. The property was left to "Leach" Zanoni, Ernest's son. "Leach's" real name was Lecio, pronounced Lee-Chay-O. When he was a boy, his friend had trouble pronouncing his name and decided to call him "Leach." He carried that name until his death. "Leach" held the property until the 1930's, when he could no longer pay the taxes. Ownership reverted to the county. The county sold it for back taxes to R. M. Andreatta in September of 1946. In 1947, Andreatta quit-claimed the property back to George Zanoni, nephew of Ernest Zanoni. Again the taxes were not paid and the county issued a tax deed to Frank B. Bostock for a $1,849 tax bid.

Fig. 53 Former Zanoni-Pedroni Florence Saloon, now the Bent Elbow Restaurant—1986. Allan Bird Photo.

Today, Effie Andreatta and her son Mike own and operate the property as the Bent Elbow Restaurant, catering to the tourist traffic during the summer months.

CHAPTER SIXTEEN
THE BON TON

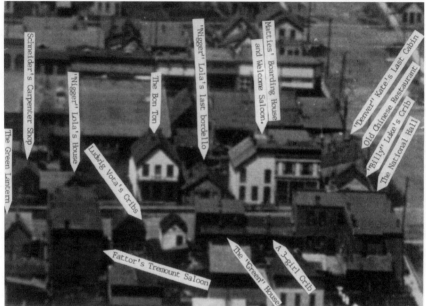

Fig. 54 1914 photo blow-up of the west side of Blair Street between 11th and 12th streets showing the Bon Ton, along with other houses on the "line." Eddie Lorenzon Photo.

The Bon Ton, one of Silverton's larger bordellos, located two doors south of the Matties Boarding House, was built during the summer of 1884 by Robert Roberts. This was another barrack-style building which predominated in early-day Silverton.

MABLE PIERCE

Roberts rented the building to a woman by the name of Miss Mable Pierce. Mable was the Madame of the house. The first mention of Mable Pierce was in the December 4, 1884, edition of the _Silverton Democrat_. The building caught fire and the following comments were reported by the paper:

CHAPTER SIXTEEN

The building occupied by Miss Mable Pierce, 557 Blair Street, was the scene of an incipient conflagration on Sunday evening. A coal oil lamp exploded which caused dire consternation among the parties present. By herculean effort the flames were extinguished. The fire department was not called out as the ladies connected a hose to their reservoir, which was luckily filled with plenty of water. The loss was slight.

Mable was constantly having trouble with her "girls." During the year 1885, Mable filed a court complaint against Bessie Smith, one of her "soiled doves." On or about January 25, 1885, Bessie Smith obtained $29 on false pretenses using all of her clothing and wearing apparel for collateral. After repaying only $5 of this amount, Bessie broke into the storage area and stole her clothes back. This crime was tried in the district court of San Juan County. Bessie had to put up a $300 bond for a $24 case. The case was tried and the court "could find no indictment."

On February 4, 1885, Mable Pierce sued Jessie Carter for the same crime. Jessie was defended by J. W. Cory, the Blair Street attorney, and was released on the grounds that the prosecution had failed to establish the venue. The case was discharged.

On May 20, 1885, the town hall records show that Mable Pierce brought suit against Jessie Carroll for disturbing the peace. In this case, the defendant, Jessie, pleaded guilty and was fined $5 plus cost, for a total of $5.35.

Mable Pierce continued to operate one of the larger bordellos on Blair Street for several years. She acquired enough money by 1889 to purchase the land and building from Robert Roberts for $1300. On September 25, 1890, she leased the building to Louisa Crawford, Jack Matties' future wife, for $100 a month rent, except for the months of February and March, when the rent was reduced to $50 a month.

In March of 1892 and again in September, Mable Pierce borrowed a total of $1400 from the local blacksmith, Henry Sherman, using the house and land as collateral. She must have married Henry Sherman as the 1894 tax rolls show the land assessed to a

Mable Sherman. In 1897 the property was assessed to D. J. Monteith. How Monteith acquired the property is not known. In 1899 the land reverted to E. L. Roberts, the local hardware and second-hand store operator. Roberts acquired the land through a sheriff's deed from a judgment decree against the administrator of the estate of M. E. Monteith. He paid $1265.15 for the lot and building.

DOTTIE WATSON

On May 15, 1899, E. L. Roberts issued a warranty deed for building and lot to Dottie Watson for $3200. Dottie also purchased:

17	Carpets for rooms.
1	Stair carpet.
9	Bedroom sets of three pieces each.
9	Bed Springs.
9	Mattresses.
2	Parlor suits of furniture.
4	Heating stoves.
21	Window shades.
1	Mirror 18" X 40".

Thus we have a description of the furnishings of one of the major bordellos. In April 1900, Dot Watson borrowed $2100 from Mrs. Mary Kloster in the form of four notes, three for $500 and one for $600, using the property as collateral. The same day she paid off her mortgage to E. L. Roberts. A month later, on May 19, Dottie Watson was brought before Judge McNutt and tried for insanity. She was declared insane and taken to the insane asylum at Pueblo. The doctors wired back to Silverton with the news that Dottie was suffering from "softening of the brain," and would probably only live sixty days at the most. Apparently she was suffering from the same disease that killed Al Capone, syphilis of the brain.

Needless to say, Dottie defaulted on her loans from Mrs. Kloster and the court awarded the property to Mrs. Kloster on July 23, 1900. The property remained in the Kloster family for years and was a popular gambling house and bordello through the 1920's. It is not known when the Bon Ton last operated, probably the late 1930's. On October 30, 1937, Lola Daggett, known as "Nigger" Lola, issued a warranty deed to lots 19, 20, and 21, block 29 to Mary Kloster. The Bon Ton was on lot 20. What interest Lola had in the Bon Ton is not known, as the court house records never listed her as an owner.

In the late 1930's, Tom Savage remembers the Bon Ton as being a restaurant and rooming house. The last occupant of the Bon Ton was a man who was known as Cornuto, which is Tyrolean for "a man who steals another man's wife." His real name was Emilio Pedot. During the 1920's Emilio worked at the Sunnyside Mine and was remembered for his photographic memory. He was well educated and spoke four languages fluently. He could read a book and then recite it, word for word. He frequently packed the room with eager listeners when he entertained his fellow miners with his stories. During his last years, Emilio lived alone in the old Bon Ton. John Matties remembers his living quarters as being "filthy." Emilio Pedot died in 1945. Shortly after his death, the Bon Ton burned to the ground.

Fig. 55 Former Silverton Mountain Pottery located on site of Bon Ton Gambling Hall and Bordello. New train shop opened in 1993. 1987. Allan Bird Photo.

CHAPTER SEVENTEEN
THE NATIONAL HALL

Formerly the Palace Hall

Fig. 56 1949 photo of the National Hall during the filming of the motion picture "Ticket to Tomahawk." Balcony and signs were built for movie set. "Jew" Fanny lived in rooms below Hotel Esmeralda Sign. Southeast corner of 12th and Blair streets. Don Stott Photo.

JANE BOWEN AGAIN

The original Palace Hall was built by Jane Bowen in August of 1892. After William Bowen's death, Jane sold her original Blair Street dance hall to Joe Sartore and bought the vacant lot across the street on the southeast corner of 12th and Blair streets. She purchased the lot with two $350 notes, one from George Barnes, trustee, due October 29, 1892; and the other from George Davis due July 1, 1893. She gave the construction contract to George Davis.

CHAPTER SEVENTEEN

He completed the original structure, which occupied only the corner lot, during the week ending August 13, 1892. She bought the bar fixtures from the American Saloon Fixture Company, Chicago, Illinois. She signed a note for $450, at six percent interest, to be paid in full within six months. The note was made out to Jane Bowen—Widow. The saloon was furnished with the following fixtures:

    1 Counter 16 feet long, oak, style 'Congress.'
    1 Back Bar 14 feet long, oak, style 'Congress.'
    1 Tank, zinc lined.
    1 Window for house.
    1 Mirror 'Congress' style, 40 X 70 inch center
      mirror plate and bevel arch top. End plates, frame oak.
    1 Arm rail and brackets.
    1 Foot rail and brackets.
    1 Beer Cooler, oak, style 'Polar.'

Before her building was completed, she purchased a piano for $450 from the Knight-Campbell Music Company, the final payment to be made in March of 1894.

She held a grand ball for the entire town of Silverton a few days after completion of the new building. The *Silverton Standard* commented that the elite of Silverton attended and then followed with the statement: "The lack of space prevents us from giving the names." In other words, the "elite" of Silverton should not be attending dances in Jane Bowen's new bordello. The new Palace Hall became a popular place with the frequenters of Blair Street.

Even with her new success, life for Jane Bowen was not easy. In January 1893, Mr. John Louis, Jane Bowen's nephew who arrived in America only three weeks past, died in the dance hall. He left a wife and nine children, "in very poor circumstances," in England. In April 1895, she was caring for another nephew from England when the two got into a small misunderstanding. The boy retaliated by putting carbolic acid in the food being served Jane and the girls of the house. She shipped him out on the next train. In February 1898, Jane Bowen's 28-year-old adopted daughter, Emily Bowen, committed suicide in Denver by taking "Rough on

Rats." She had been in poor health and was living in St. Catherine's Home.

In 1893, Jane purchased the adjoining lot to the south from Mrs. Murphy, owner of the Silverton Hotel. About 1895, she built a large addition onto the Palace Hall on the newly purchased lot. She used this new building as a bordello.

Immediately after the death of her adopted daughter in February of 1898, Jane decided to give up the business for a while and return to her home in England. On February 28, she leased the Palace Hall to Jack Matties, who owned the Welcome Saloon across the street. The lease was to extend from March 1, 1898, to March 1, 1900. The rent was to be $75 per month during the summer months and $50 during the winter season. It became known as Jack Matties' Dance Hall during this period. The first mention of Jack's new dance hall was in the May 6, 1899, *Silverton Standard*:

> Thursday night Charles Payne was stabbed by Jesse Shields in Jack Matties' Dance Hall. Two wounds, neither of which is considered dangerous, were inflicted. Payne bled like a butcher, was brought up town and properly cared for. One puncture was just over the heart and the other in the left arm, above the elbow. Woman, lovely woman was the cause of the row.

Again, On October 21, 1899, the *Standard* reported:

> Wednesday night May Crawford, one of the inmates of Jack Matties' Dance Hall, while laboring under the influence of too much booze, swallowed a big dose of carbolic acid, probably with a view of neutralizing the effects of the red liquor. Dr. Ingersoll was called and with the aid of a stomach pump soon put the girl to rights.

After Jack Matties' lease expired in 1900, the property was leased to Albert Swanson who occupied the hall until Jane's return. During the week ending February 15, 1902, a letter arrived from England announcing that the "Sage Hen" would be returning to start up the Palace Dance Hall. Upon her return, the liquor license was transferred from Albert Swanson back to Jane Bowen. The March 1, 1902, *Silverton Standard* printed the following review of her return:

THE NATIONAL HALL

Once again will the Palace Dance Hall echo with the strains of music, the tread of dancing feet and the clink of the inspiring schooner; once again will a familiar voice admonish the uproarous throng to "lift the room off me 'ouse." For the 'Sage Hen,' nee Mrs. Jane Bowen, has returned from London after an absence of about two years to conduct the frivilous resort.

Jane Bowen returned and announced in the paper that "My 'ouse 'as received a new coat of paint and now I will 'ave a grand hopening." Shortly before her "grand hopening," she was arrested for wearing indecent dress on the street. She made a trip to the city council meeting to ask "why she was not allowed to come out on the street and look at her "hone 'ouse." She was informed that she could if she would dress up for the occasion. A month later, "Aunt Jane", as she was often called, returned to the council meeting and informed the board that she was ready to pay her dance hall license, provided however, that sporting houses using dancing rooms in connection with their houses also be made to pay a dance hall license.

The June 27, 1903, issue of the _Silverton Standard_ printed the following invitation:

'Aunt Jane' wishes to inform the public that she has again taken charge of the dance hall at the southeast corner of 12th and Blair streets and will conduct the same good old fashioned way. Good music, fine floor and 'Aunt Jane' says 'boys from the 'ills hare hinvited to call 'round hand take ha glass hat 'er hexpense.

This notice would indicate that she closed the Palace during the winter months. This was her practice when she operated the old dance hall across the street.

Jane Bowen retired some time before February of 1905. The paper printed the story of Johnnie Hill, who slipped and fell, dislocating his hip while carrying water to the building "formerly occupied" by the "Sage Hen's" dancers. They commented that "Aunt Jane, the retired dance hall manager," had him under her care.

CHAPTER SEVENTEEN

JOHN ORELLA'S AND VIGILIO VALDAN'S NATIONAL HALL

On July 8, 1905, Jane Bowen sold the Palace Hall to Peter Orella, owner of the Standard Bottling Works, for $3500. The August 5, 1905, _Silverton Standard_ printed the following notice of their grand opening:

> John Orella (Peter's brother) and V. Valdan have opened a first class saloon in the 'Aunt Jane' building on the southeast corner of Blair and 12th streets. The boys propose running a first-class resort and they extend a general invitation for everybody to give them a call.

In November of 1905, Peter Orella signed a formal lease to John Orella, Vigilio Valdan, and Joe Louisa to extend from July 1, 1905, until June 30, 1909. The rent was to be a total of $1920 at the rate of $40 per month. Part of the lease requirements were that, "the lawn be clipped and that they obey all laws."

The Christmas day edition of the Standard published the short notice that "A new resort—an academy for old dancers—has been reorganized at the 'Aunt Jane' Dance Hall, and will be known as the National Saloon and Hall."

JOE CORAZZA'S NATIONAL HALL

A month before the above lease was to expire in 1909, Peter Orella sold the property to Joe and Santina Corazza for $5000. The Corazzas paid $1100 down and took out a $3900 mortgage from Pete Orella.

The Corazzas prospered in the National Hall. Mrs. Corazza made a practice of returning to her home in Tyrol, Austria. When she returned to America, she would smuggle diamonds, hiding them in her knitting yarn. She became the local under-cover diamond agent for Silverton.

On Saturday night, January 27, 1918, Joe Corazza died shortly before the hour of 12 o'clock. Joe Corazza was born in Tyrol, Austria in 1878. He moved to Silverton in 1906. Before he ran the National Hall he worked in the mines. The cause of his death was pneumonia.

Mrs. Corazza continued to operate the National Hall until 1929. During the years that they operated the hall, the Corazzas purchased lot 3, the site of "Fatty" Collin's old saloon and bordello. On October 9, 1929, Mrs. Corraza sold the three lots, with all buildings, to Mike Serra. During the 1930's and 1940's the property passed though several owners. Times changed for the worse. By the mid 1950's, the taxes were allowed to lapse. On January 2, 1957, San Juan County issued a tax deed to Frank Bostock for $1172 for the three lots. The buildings had probably been demolished before the tax sale. Several "old timers" have said that the large snow storm of 1952 collapsed portions of the roof of the original building. The structure was standing in 1954 and probably demolished in the late 1950's.

During the late 1940's and early 1950's the National Hall was the scene of several Hollywood movie sets.

Fig. 57 1954 view of the National Hall. The train stops next to this location.
Ruth Gregory Collection.

THE NATIONAL HALL

From about 1935 until the time she left Silverton in 1948, "Jew" Fanny lived in the ground floor rooms located in the south wing of the National Hall. This was the last whorehouse in Silverton.

Fig. 58 The Tomaselli sisters, Annie (left) and Mary (right) in front of the National Hall. About 1928. The Tomaselli family operated a boarding house on the northwest corner of 11th and Blair streets. "Jew" Fanny's rooms were to right of Mary's shoulder. John and Joe Matties Photo.

Fig. 59 Joe Corazza—1878-1918, owner of the National Hall from 1909 until his death. Mrs. Corazza continued business until 1929. Photo taken from his gravestone—damaged by vandals. Allan Bird Photo.

CHAPTER EIGHTEEN
DIAMOND BELLE

Fig. 60 1914 photo showing the Diamond Belle Dance Hall and Bordello along with the other buildings on the "line" along Blair Street between 12th and 13th streets. The names of the buildings are listed as they were commonly known in later years, for example, in 1914, the Laundry was Billy Luke's Dance Hall. Eddie Lorenzon Photo.

The Diamond Belle Dance Hall and bordello was located on the east side of Blair Street.[23] two doors north of 12th Street. The property was originally sold on September 14, 1880, by G. T. Stauton to Mrs. Ellen Murry for $1000. This would suggest that there was a rather large, early bordello on the site. By 1885, the property was assessed at only $300. Either Mrs. Murry paid too much for the property or there was a large building that was possibly destroyed by fire and later replaced with a small crib.

By 1885, John Wingate owned the property and the small building. His name appears on the tax rolls until 1890, when the building was assessed at only $100. By 1893, the owner of the lot was unknown to the county taxing authorities.

LOUISA CRAWFORD AND JACK MATTIES

In 1895, Jack Matties was shown as the owner. The following year, 1896, Louisa Crawford owned the crib and the assessment doubled from $100 to $200. On June 24, 1897, Louisa Crawford sold the lot and building to Jack Matties, along with lots 22 and 23, block 29, the site of the Matties' Boarding House and Welcome Saloon, for $2000.[24] Again, on October 15, 1898, Jack Matties issued a warranty deed back to Louisa Crawford for the future Diamond Belle site for $1.

LOUISA MAURELL

On November 2, 1898, a French woman by the name of Louisa Maurell, issued a note to Jack Matties for $250 for the lot and building. She moved into the small crib and set up shop. Five months later she paid off her mortgage to Matties and became the owner of the property. Louisa Maurell had a sister, Marie. Both girls had run a brothel in Ouray and owned the property. On November 17, 1899, they mortgaged the new Silverton property along with their property in Ouray to a Marshal Orendorf for $1000 due October 22, 1900. With this capital they hired a few girls and expanded their business on Blair Street.

In April, 1902, Louisa tore down the old crib and hired a local carpenter, Charles Dale, to begin building the large wooden frame, barracks-style building, which she named the Diamond Belle. The building was 24 feet wide and 80 feet long, two stories high. It contained twelve rooms for the "dancers" above the dance hall, and rooms and a dance hall with a hardwood finish on the main floor. The May 10, 1902, *Silverton Standard* described the grand opening as follows:

> At the grand opening of the new Honkytonk on Blair Street last Saturday night many were the comments on the new resort—the elaborate bar fixtures and bric-a-brac. Lack of space crowds out the names of those in attendance, and may our readers forbear the absence of the news until next week.

139

CHAPTER EIGHTEEN

This was the newspapers idea of a local joke. Patrons of whorehouses were not anxious to have their names printed in the paper.

The opening of the Diamond Belle coincided with the "Chinese problem" in Silverton. The labor unions had ordered the townspeople of Silverton to boycott all Chinese business establishments. Word was being circulated that Louisa and Marie Maurell's girls were eating at one of the local Chinese restaurants. The two women were quick to publish the following denial in the May 1, 1902, _Silverton Standard_:

> At the instigation of envious competitors, a report is being circulated that the boarders of the Diamond Belle Dance Hall are patronizing the Chinese restaurants in Silverton, upon which a boycott has been declared. The purpose of this mischievous falsehood is, of course, to put us in an attitude of hostility toward the unions. We wish to say most emphatically that our establishment has never patronized a boycotted firm, Mongolian or Causcasian, and never will.
>
> (Signed)
> Louisa and Maria Maurell
> Diamond Dance Hall

In the latter part of May, 1902, a Belgian blacksmith by the name of Albert Van Dereyken arrived in Silverton with $170 that he had saved over the past year. The poor soul could speak only French and was overwhelmed with joy when he discovered that Louisa Maurell, the French proprietress of the Diamond Belle could speak his language. He was so happy that he began to spend some of his hard-earned money on drinks. He soon became drunk and the women put him to bed in a semi-conscious state. When he awoke the next morning, all of his money had been stolen. He panicked and approached Louisa, pleading his case. He soon learned what the phrase, "harder than a whore's heart," meant. She claimed that he had spent all of his money on champagne. He said that he may have been drunk but he remembered buying only four bottles. She told him to get out, whereupon he pulled a pocket knife from his pocket and stabbed her twice, once in the back below the waist and once in the hip or thigh. The wound was about two and one-half inches deep and two inches long, but was not considered serious. The Belgian was arrested and allowed to enter a plea of simple assault. He received a sentence of twenty days in jail.

The miners didn't appreciate this type of treatment to one of their own and business began to fall off for the Maurells shortly after the Belle opened. In June, one month after her grand opening, she had to borrow $2000 from Peter Orella at one percent per month interest. Tension among the women was probably rather high, resulting in fights among the "girls." On September 6, 1902, the _Silverton Standard_ reported the fight between Pearl Marshall and Louisa Maurell. The story read as follows:

> It was slightly cool in the court room the morning of the 3rd and Judge Hodges was not feeling his best when Pearl Marshall, alias "Gip" stepped before the altar of justice (by request) and pleaded guilty to the charge of fighting. Pearl winked one eye (the other was too black to budge) and the judge said 'total $14.75.'

> Louisa Maurell was called next to answer to the same charge and with an assuring air said 'not guilty.' The judge would not stand for the bluff and said '$10 and costs, full amount $19.75.' Louisa requested that she be confined in a secluded spot owned by the city. While on her way to the bastille, Louise changed her mind and donated the sum to the city funds.

The following week her piano player dropped dead from a supposed heart attack, "occasioned by unusual drinking." He was forty-eight years old and a native of England. He had been playing piano in Silverton for the past eight years. By December 1902, Louisa Maurell was broke. She sold the Belle to Fred McIlmoyle who "will endeavor to make the unsuccessful venture of the past supervisors pay." (_Silverton Standard_) He proposed to change the name to the Diamond Belle Amusement Center. As soon as McIlmoyle had taken charge of the Belle than he was arrested for trying to kill his wife. The paper attributed his actions to insanity caused by too many "mixed" drinks. McIlmoyle had a partner by the name of J. A. Doucet, who dissolved their partnership after the wife-killing attempt.

CHAPTER EIGHTEEN

Soon Louisa Maurell had her building back when McIlmoyle defaulted on his mortgage. In April 1903, she borrowed $3000 from the Schirmer Insurance and Investment Company for three years, to be repaid quarterly. She used the lot and building as collateral.

She apparently leased the dance hall to a Thomas Grosso. During the period of the lease she kept a hand in the management of the Belle. On New Year's Eve, 1903, she gave a grand ball in which the entire town was invited. No mention was made in the papers as to who attended. In April 1904, the Diamond Belle again made the *Silverton Standard*. This time a "poor unfortunate inmate," Maggie Crowley died of heart failure brought on by excessive drink.

Louisa Maurell soon learned that the way to make money in the dance hall and bordello business was to borrow money from unsuspecting suckers. Before she had paid her debt to the Schirmer Insurance and Investment company, she took out another loan for $3000 at eight percent interest per year on April 10, 1905, from the German American Trust Company, using the same collateral. This was a two-year loan. What she did with the money is not known; however, on August 26, 1905, she formalized her lease of the Diamond Belle to Thomas Grosso for three years ending on August 1, 1906. He had been leasing the property for the past two years and evidently she was just getting down to putting it on paper. He was to pay her a total rent of $4500 at the rate of $125 per month, beginning August 1, 1903.

In May 1906, the paper reported that Tom Gross, (Grosso) the proprietor of the Diamond Belle, was reported missing while he ostensibly was on a horseback ride to Ouray. A search was begun and his horse, with a rifle and knife attached to the saddle, was found. The first theory of his disappearance was that he had attempted to cross the river and drowned. After thoroughly searching the river, this theory was abandoned. It was finally decided that he was actually skipping the country to avoid paying his creditors. The *Standard* reported that, "he had been reported seen in Durango, Ouray, and a dozen other places since his demise. Meanwhile grass is sprouting around his old business stand."

142

THE DIAMOND BELLE

Again the management of the Diamond Belle reverted to Louisa Maurell. On May 24, 1907, she deeded the land and building to the Schirmer Insurance Company as settlement for her old debt. The insurance company owned the Belle for about three years. On November 11, 1910, Godfried Schirmer sold the Belle to John Orella. John Orella had recently operated the National Hall for his brother Peter. Orella operated the Diamond Belle until May 8, 1922, when he deeded half of the property to Joe Orella, probably his son. Joe Orella promptly deeded his half of the property to his wife Castanga Orella. The Diamond Belle remained in the Orella family for many years.

By 1928, the property was under the control of Frank Walisky. The January 14, 1928, *Silverton Standard* printed the story of the safe robbery at the Belle:

ROBS SAFE AND SEEKS NEW LOCATION

Some time Sunday night after the close of business, Frank Williams, who has been in the Silverton district for a short time and was employed as a caretaker at the Diamond Belle resort on Blair Street, got the notion into his head that he needed some extra money and therefore proceeded to bust into the safe in the house and abstract some $250 therefrom and on the next day make his way to Durango. He had been in the Smelter City but a short time when he was picked up by an officer there upon the advice of Sheriff M. H. Doud, of San Juan, and landed in the jail to await developments. When he was taken into custody he was under the influence of liquor and when he was searched he was found to have some ninety odd dollars of the plunder in his pockets. Whether or not he will be returned to Silverton is not known, he may decide to go before the Court in Durango and plead guilty and eliminate all necessary procedures and be sentenced by Judge Searcy, who is the man of the bench for this district, at that place. The party who was relieved of the $250 is known here as Frank Walisky.

Williams had been posing around here as a boxer and but recently gave an exhibition here at a smoker, and seemed to be a very quiet sort of man, but you can never tell in such events just what is in store.

The Diamond Belle operated as a bordello well into the 1930's. George Sitter managed the Belle for a period of time during this period. He had been "married" to Pearl Eastman, who died during the flu epidemic. Later he was Frances Belmont's "man", and finally he married Laura Philips. He also served as a pall bearer for "21" Pearl. According to John Matties, "he was a real rounder."

According to Louis Dalla's notes, Bertha "Kate" Starr, Billy Deboyd, and Rose Rody worked at 1216 Blair Street, the address of the Diamond Belle. When Mary Swanson was a young girl, she remembered, Kate Starr looked about six feet tall. "Sheeny" Pearl Miller also worked in the Diamond Belle. According to Jim Hook, Sr., when Pearl was older she "was as wide as she was tall." Mrs. Orella repurchased the property and had the building demolished in the 1940's.

Fig. 61 The Diamond Belle Dance Hall about 1940.
Jim Bell Photo.

---

23 The Diamond Belle was located on the east side of Blair Street, two doors north of the present Arcade Gift Shop.

24 Matties' Saloon and Boarding house was on the west side of Blair Street, south of 12th Street.

THE
MONTE CARLO

Presently the "Hitching Post"

Fig. 62 1954 photo of Mattivi's Monte Carlo Gambling Hall and Saloon. Mattivi's Stable at right of brick building. See Fig. 60 for the location of the Monte Carlo. Signs from movie "Run for Cover" with James Cagney. Ruth Gregory Collection.

The Monte Carlo was a gambling hall and bordello built in 1907. The building was of brick construction. It is located on the east side of Blair Street about midway between 12th and 13th streets. Early records show that lot 7 contained a small building, probably a crib, as early as 1882. It was owned by W. J. Grow, a local butcher, and was assessed at $300 in 1882. In 1884, Grow sold the lot and building to Mr. N. E. Slaymaker, a local real estate broker. Sometime between 1887 and 1893, the property was sold to E. L. Roberts, the hardware dealer who invested in Blair Street bordellos. Both Slaymaker and Roberts leased the crib out to independent women over the years. In 1901, the building was removed, probably from decay. The taxes were transferred to Mrs. Emma Roberts, E. L. Roberts' wife.

145

Fig. 63 Photo showing the Monte Carlo and the old wooden bordello to the south. About 1912. Wooden building destroyed in 1913. Denver Pub. Lib. West. Hist. Col. Photo.

MATTIVI'S

On January 8, 1907, Emma Roberts sold lots 7 and 8, along with 2 feet of lot 9, block 19 to John Mattivi for $1700. This would indicate that Roberts actually built the present two-story brick building on lot 7 in 1906. A large frame bordello existed since 1901 on lot 8, to the south of the brick Monte Carlo, . The Mattivi's bought both structures in the deal. In August 1907, John Mattivi borrowed $500 from August Fast, another Silverton real estate broker, using the lots and buildings for collateral. Again, in October, he borrowed $1000 from Mr. Louis Sartore for one year at eight percent interest. By January 1908, Mattivi had repaid his loans, indicating that business must have been good. The frame bordello on lot 8 was either destroyed by fire or torn down in late 1912 or early 1913. A small residence was built by the Mattivi's near the rear of this lot. The Mattivi family operated the gambling hall and bordello until July 7, 1924, when John Mattivi leased the property to Nick Spolarich from April 23, 1924 to February 23, 1925, for a total rent of $300, payable at the rate of $30 per month. The lease specified that it was "for the two story brick building, known as the Monte Carlo."

THE MONTE CARLO

By February 19, 1929, the property was owned by Louis Mattivi, probably John Mattivi's son. He transferred the deed to Lena Mattivi Popovich and Rosa Mattivi. In June 1929, Luigia Mattivi leased the front room of the Monte Carlo building to W. W. Lancaster and Joe Ocamica. The lease was to run from June 7, 1929, to December 7, 1929. The total rent was to be $600, at the rate of $100 per month. It was specified in the lease that the room was "not to be used for the manufacture or disposal of intoxicating liquors." This was a clause included in all Prohibition-era leases. Bootleg whiskey was sold in the Monte Carlo. Most of the saloons and bordellos on Blair Street were easy sources of moonshine whiskey.

Annie Smith recalls, "Mattivi's was a 'hook-shop', 'Jew' Rose worked there." Corky Scheer claimed, "There were quite a number of girls in there. They were all young and tender. I've been thrown out of all of them."

On December 1, 1931, Rosa Mattivi and Lena Popovich issued a warranty deed to Luigia Mattivi for the Monte Carlo and adjoining lots. The hall was run as a gambling den and bordello until about 1935.

After the war, Tom Hadden bought the property in August 1946. He sold it to Rosa Dorigatti and Adelina Holgrem in 1946. In 1959, the building was purchased by Frank Bostock who sold it to Vern and Eloise Parker in 1961. In 1949, the building was used as a bank in the movie "Run for Cover" starring James Cagney. A false front was constructed on the building. During a bank robbery scene, the false front was blown off with explosives. In 1978 structural problems developed on the second floor which required the removal and replacement of the original brick front of the building. The new front was plain by comparison to the original ornate brickwork.

Today the building houses Allen Parker's glass-blowing establishment.

Fig. 64 The Monte Carlo in 1986. Now occupied by Allen Parker's Glass Blowing Studio. Notice the new brick front on the building. Allan Bird Photo.

CHAPTER TWENTY
FRATTOR'S TREMOUNT SALOON

Fig. 65 Fattor's Tremount Saloon and Bordello. "Big Tillie" Fattor standing at left. Celeste Fattor, "Big Tillie's" husband, in white apron. Women "inmates" peering out of upstairs windows. About 1910. Jim Bell Collection.

Fattor's Tremount Saloon was located on the east side of Blair, about midway between 11th and 12th streets. The first building to be constructed on the site was a small Chinese laundry, built by H. O. Wing in 1882. The land was sold in 1884 to a Mr. Adsit, an early Silverton pioneer. The small building was assessed to Mr. Adsit, at least through 1887. By 1893, the county listed the owner as "unknown."

In 1894 it was listed as "unknown, now Spider's." and assessed at $25. Spider was the local nickname for W. S. Hung, a Chinese laundryman. "Spider" operated his laundry until February 1902, when he was shot at by a mob attempting to rid Silverton of the Chinese. In an attempt to salvage something of his possessions, he borrowed $300 from the owner of the Hub Saloon, Jack Slattery. The Hub was located in the Grand Hotel (Grand Imperial). On May 14, 1902, Hung gave Slattery a quit-claim deed to his property for an additional $50. Hung left Silverton forever. Slattery probably leased the building as a small crib.

Fig. 65 a. Matilda "Big Tilly" Fattor at right. Other woman unknown. ca. 1910. Mr. & Mrs. Kenneth Jakino Photo.

"BIG TILLY"

On January 31, 1907, Jack Slattery sold the land and crib to Matilda Wenden Fattor. She was affectionately known as "Big Tilly" to the natives of Silverton. She was a large-framed woman, weighing between 300 and 400 pounds. She married Celeste Fattor, a man about half her size. "Tilly" actually owned the land and building until June 21, 1911, when she deeded half of the property to Celeste. "Big Tilly" served as the Madame and bouncer of the bordello.

Annie Smith related how, as a small girl, she and her friends would peek through the back door keyhole to watch the girls dancing. She claimed that "Tilly" would make an annual trip to the Mayo Clinic to have some of her fat removed surgically. The bordello was upstairs and contained fourteen beds. This was large for Blair Street.

On March 19, 1917, Celeste Fattor sold the building to his brother Louis for $2000. Louis had worked as the Tremount's bartender. On August 29, 1917, Louis sold back to Tilly "lot 7, block 30, No. 1134 Blair Street. Fourteen beds plus all other furniture."

"Big Tilly" contracted pneumonia. After a week of sickness, she died January 25, 1918. She was 42 years old. "Tilly" was born in Sweden on April 11, 1875. The February 3, 1918, _Silverton Standard_ printed the following obituary:

MRS. C. FATTOR DIES OF PNEUMONIA
Died Last Friday

For the past sixteen years, Mrs. Fattor has lived in Silverton, and for years conducted the Tremount place of business with her husband. She was a woman who made many friends. She was charitable and kind and when death claimed her as a victim, regardless of everything, death robbed many of this county of a real friend.

Mrs. Fattor was born in Sweden in the year 1875. When a young girl she came to this country and with her father she located in Georgetown in 1888. When she was 18 years of age she moved to Ouray and until sixteen years ago she called that city her home. Since then she has been a resident of Silverton. In 1905 she was married to Celeste Fattot at Durango. Before her marriage she was Matilda Wendin.

Most everyone in San Juan knew Mrs. Fattor and her acquaintances were all her friends.

Note: The following day, Joe Corazza, owner of the National Hall, died of pneumonia.

The above praises were verified by the "old timers" who knew her. No one ever said a bad word about her. She died in the upstairs of the Tremount Saloon. It took six men to carry her body down the stairs. A special coffin, constructed by joining two regular size coffins together, had to be built to hold her remains. She was buried at Springfield, Massachusetts.

Shortly after "Tilly's" death, Celeste leased the saloon and bordello to two of his inmates, Lena Cummings and Georgia Mills. The lease was to run from March 1, 1918 to March 1, 1919 with a total rent of $750 to be paid at the rate of $187.50 every quarter.

Celeste returned to his home in Italy and brought back a new wife. He continued to operate the Tremount until August 3, 1925, when he sold the property to Louisa Visintin for $3500. Louisa held the property for less than a year. After her short duration of ownership, the Tremount went through a complicated series of sales, with several people buying and selling half-interests. In 1929, Gio Bari ended up owning the property. He borrowed $2600 from Mrs. Corazza, using the property as collateral. A clause in the loan agreement stated that the property, "is not to be used for prostitution."

The Great Depression struck in October 1929, and even the red light district of Silverton felt the pinch. Gio Bari was forced to seek a loan in December 1931. Mrs. Sam Eccher loaned him $2000 using the property as collateral. Bari could not repay the loan and

Fig. 66 1954 Photo. Old Tremount Saloon was a liquor store in the mid-1930's. There was a small bar in the rear of the building. Building burned January 16, 1968. Signs were for movie set. Ruth Gregory Collection.

the property was awarded to Mrs. Eccher in 1933. The building was used as a liquor store with a bar in the back. The upstairs was converted into a rooming house during much of the 1930's and 1940's. Mrs. Eccher retained the building until 1952.

According to "Leach" Zanoni, Frank Bostock purchased the building and opened the first Bent Elbow Restaurant. He sold the restaurant to Effie Andreatta who continued to operate the business. This building was destroyed by fire on January 16, 1968. After the fire, Effie Andreatta moved her restaurant into the old Zanoni-Pedroni Florence Saloon, a few doors to the south, where it remains today. (1993)

Fig. 67 Ornate Bar in Fattor's Tremount Saloon. Date unknown. San Juan Co. Hist. Soc. Photo.

Spitoon - 1895   *Cuspidor - Plain - 1895*   *Cuspidor - "Tip-proof" - 1895*

CHAPTER TWENTY-ONE
THE TREE TOP

Fig. 68 1914 photo showing location of the Tree Top Crib. West side of Blair Street, just north of 12th Street. Eddie Lorenzon Photo.

The Tree Top, a small, four-girl crib located next door, to the north of the Laundry.[25] The 1881 tax rolls show that the property was owned by Alice Norris and assessed $350 for both land and buildings. Alice Norris sold the crib to George Bradford, one of the owners of the Exchange Livery Stable, in 1882. Bradford owned the crib for eleven years when he sold it to George Roberts in 1893. On May 26, 1894, Louis Sartore purchased the land from Roberts for $200. In 1896, Joe Sartore, Louis Sartore's brother, owned the property jointly with Ludwig Vota, operator of Ludwig's Dance Hall next door. They used it as part of their bordello.

THE TREE TOP

The girls who worked in the dance hall would use this building for their customers "after the dance." Judging from the tax assessment, Sartore and Vota doubled the size of the building in 1898, when the assessed value jumped from $25 to $50. Sartore and Vota owned the property until their deaths. On July 1, 1937, Philip Sartore, Joe Sartore's nephew, and Mary Vota, sold the land to Mrs. Louisa Anesi.

Jim Hook, Sr. remembers the name "Tree Top." Annie Smith, referred to it as the "Mexican whorehouse." Few of the "old timers" could recall that this establishment had a name, they remembered it as being just a four-girl crib.

The March 26, 1904, _Silverton Standard_ described the following incident which probably took place in the Tree Top:

Tuesday night at about 8 o'clock W. H. Charlton, who had been employed as cook in the Vienna Cafe, swallowed two ounces of chloral hydrate and stretched himself out for a long sleep on a bed in one of the frame shacks just above Luke's Dance Hall, where lives the object of his adoration, a woman of the town, whose stage name is 'Florence.' Medical assistance was summoned, and, by the strenuous exertion of two of our physicians, the poison was pumped out of the man, although for several hours afterward it was thought that he could not pull through. The herbic treatment, resorted to by the medical gentlemen, ultimately had the desired effect, and, at this writing, Wednesday, Charlton is said to be out of danger. On the night of the attempted suicide his employers discharged him, he leaving the place flat broke. Evidently he had listened too long to the songs of the siren, while basking in the sunlight of her smiles, to pack very much loose change in his jeans. He is a man of family, having a wife and one child who were expected in from Denver on the night of the rash act.

It is not known how long the Tree Top operated but like most of the others, its demise was probably in the late 1930's. The building was visible in a 1954 photo but has long since been demolished.

---

[25] The Tree Top was located on the west side of Blair Street, two lots north of 12th Street.

Fig. 69 The Mikado Saloon and Bordello, about 1940.   Door at left entered the bar, door at right the bordello.   Jim Bell Collection.

The Mikado was a small saloon, dance hall and bordello located next door to the north, of the Tree Top.[26] A small crib was built on the property in 1893 by C. M. Frazier, one of Silverton's lawyers of questionable reputation. Frazier sold the lot and building to Knute Benson about 1895. The exact date is unknown because the tax rolls listed the owner as "unknown" in 1895. In January of 1896, Knute Benson, who later built the large brick hotel and business establishment known as the Benson block,[27] sold the front 65 feet of the lot to R. A. Bretherton. Benson retained the back 35 feet of the lot for a small building which was used as a living quarters for his black porter. The December 28, 1901, *Silverton Standard* printed the story of a shooting that took place in this shack:

THE MIKADO

An affair of color (not honor) occurred Thursday night in which four colored persons, a six-shooter and four shots, figured prominently. A colored denizen of the 'row' known as Hattie, had two colored suitors. One of them by the name of Richards called on the woman at her room on Blair Street and quarreled and fought with her. She had him arrested. Homer Walker, a friend of Richards, went to the police authorities and after an understanding that Richards was to leave town in the morning, he was liberated. Richards and Walker then went down to the rooms of the colored man named Bryant who lives back of the Benson Block, and found the woman Hattie and a colored man by the name of Special in there. Special took a gun from under the bed to hit his rival Richards with. He also fired one shot at Walker, the ball passing through the fleshy part of the leg. He then ran out and fired the gun three times. Then he ran up behind the Teller House and fired another shot. Climbed up on a coal shed to avoid pursuit, jumped down again and sprained his ankle and was soon afterwards arrested behind the Commercial Hotel. The woman was also arrested and jailed. Jealousy and strong drink caused the trouble.

Note: Special later escaped from jail and was recaptured in a cabin a few miles from Silverton. He was later tried and found innocent of the shooting but was fined for breaking into the cabin and stealing food during his escape attempt.

In August of 1896, Bretherton sold the east 65 feet of the lot to Sam Staples for $300, "which includes building and furniture." A year later, Sam Staples sold the property to W. D. Watson for $200, taking a $100 loss. Watson owned the property until July 8, 1916, when he deeded it to Frank L. Watson, probably his son. The property transfer included the phrase "Love and affection to Frank Watson."

During the entire time of its existence, the building was rented out to women of the "line" and was used as a one-girl crib. On September 2, 1925, Frank Watson sold the ground to Edward Washington for $525. Watson had added a lean-to to the original building and probably increased the depth of the building. A month later, Washington sold the property to "21" Pearl Thompson for $725.

"21" PEARL

When the building acquired the name "Mikado" is not known, but "21" Pearl probably named it. Pearl Thompson was a tall, thin, attractive woman. She had a partner by the name of Frances Belmont. Together they ran the Mikado. Pearl acquired her nickname "21" because of her passion for the game of blackjack. Annie Smith related the story of how the local Catholic priest would often enjoy coming into the Mikado for a glass of wine. Frances Belmont was a staunch Catholic and Pearl was Jewish. When it came time to pay, the priest put his money on the bar and Frances tried to refuse payment. Pearl interrupted with, "his money looks like anyone else's," putting it in the cash register.

Fig. 70 "21" Pearl Thompson, owner of the Mikado. Photo taken from her gravestone—1892-1928. Allan Bird Photo.

"21" Pearl had a small dog which she treated like a child. When Corky Scheer was a young boy about ten, he and his friends would kidnap her dog and hide it in their garage. After a period of time, they would saunter past the Mikado and Pearl would come out frantically inquiring if they had seen her dog. Of course they would deny any knowledge of the dog's whereabouts. She would then offer them a reward if they could find the mutt. They would wait about an hour or two, and then return the dog. The reward was a standard $5 bill, which was a world of money to a group of small boys. The act was repeated several times a year. She never did catch on.

Frances and Pearl had an accordion player by the name of Joe Paycheck. He provided the music for the dancing. Joe later married a girl of the "line."

THE MIKADO

One of the employees of the Mikado in 1926 was "Big Billie" whose real name was Betty Wagner. She was a tall, large woman. "Billie" came to Silverton from Telluride when that town closed its red light district in 1923. On Halloween night 1926, Jim Hook, Sr. and a group of his high school friends, decided to steal the outhouse from the Mikado. Someone had stolen one the year before and placed it in front of the First National Bank with a sign that read "Second National Bank, make your deposits here." Jim and his friends enjoyed this joke so much they thought it was worth repeating. They reached the scene of their proposed crime only to find that the small building was well anchored to the ground. They put all their strength to the task and began rocking the building. In the process they made a little too much noise. "Big Billie" appeared at the back door with the admonition to "get the hell out of here you little S. O. B.s." At the same time emptying all six chambers of a 38-calibre revolver in their general direction. They never returned.

On February 13, 1928, "21" Pearl Thompson died. The cause of her death is not definitely known. Annie Smith claims she committed suicide by taking an overdose of pills. "Leach" Zanoni remembers that they found her dead in her room but the cause of death was never determined. The February 18, 1928, _Silverton Standard_ published the following obituary:

> Pearl Thompson funeral held Monday morning at the Congregational Church, with Rev. F. L. Shoemaker of the Presbyterian Church in Durango, officiating. It was a large assemblage that gathered to pay their last respects to the one that was being buried, and it has been many days since a greater wealth of floral tributes has been seen hereabouts, and in the remarks of the minister who preached the sermon, he dwelt upon the life hereafter and in doing so took the sting of death away from those who had gathered at this funeral. The pall bearers were from among friends of the deceased and were as follows: George Sitter, Tom Olson, Alex McDonald, Fritz Blackman, Tony Casserio and Henry Shields. Peace to the departed is the desire and wish of all those who knew her.

Pearl was buried in Hillside Cemetery, Silverton. Her photo is imbedded in her granite tombstone. She was thirty-six years old.

CHAPTER TWENTY-TWO

"BIG BILLIE"

"Big Billie" took over as one of the Madames of the Mikado after Pearl's death. Evidently times were hard for hookers during 1928. The San Juan County Historical Society has in its possession a letter from a prostitute in Leadville written to "Big Billie" inquiring about the prospects for work in Silverton. The letter read as follows:

> Dear Billie:
>   No doubt you will be surprised to hear from me but I heard you were there and I'm writing to ask how business is and is there a chance for an old lady to come over and go to work? There is absolutely nothing here and I want to get away from here as soon as I can for I will drive my car out of here and I want to leave before the snow gets too deep. If I can get a crib or go to work in one of the joints let me know. I wrote to Garnett and she said there wasn't any place there I could get so I guess I can still work a bit myself. Please answer at once and let me know. Must close now and put this in the mail, so, by-by (sic) and answer soon.
>   P.S. If you call you can get me at 351 after 6 p. m.
>   Mamie G.
>   200 N. 3rd St.

Jim Hook, Sr. related the story of "Big Jumbo," a "huge man" who worked as a miner at the Sunnyside Mine, Silverton's largest gold mine. Before coming to Silverton, he had worked as a sand-hog during the construction of the subways in Chicago. It seems that "Big Jumbo" was drinking in the Mikado when one of the women made the foolish mistake of insulting him. He proclaimed that:

> He didn't like this place and he was going to move the bar out into the street. He started to tug at the bar when 'Billie' got up on a chair and rapped him on the head with a blackjack. He spent the night in jail to sober up. The next morning he found that all his money was gone and he had to bum breakfast from of the cafe. He high-tailed it back to the mine where he could stay out of trouble.

Another anecdote related by Jim was the story of "Fats" Fleming, the mine superintendent of the Sunnyside. "Fats" liked his liquor and was drinking in the Mikado when one of his miners, "Shorty" Fant, came in. After a few drinks, "Shorty" got belligerent with another miner, and the two ended up in a fight. "Shorty" was promptly knocked on his fanny and as he sat in the middle of the floor in a semi-dazed condition, "Fats" yelled out to him, "Shorty, get up off your ass, you're not working for me now."

FRANCES BELMONT

A few months before her death, Pearl Thompson sold the Mikado to a W. H. Mowat for $1,000. Mowat, in turn, sold the property in March 1934, to Pearl's former partner, Frances Belmont with the provision that she was to pay the back taxes for the years 1931, 1932, and 1933. Frances had occupied the Mikado since Pearl's death.

Frances Belmont was well liked by the people of Silverton. During the depression she fed many hungry mouths with her generous donations of food to the poor and needy. Frances operated the Mikado until her death from cancer in 1936. For a while, George Sitter was her "man." She later married John Anzek.

After the death of Frances Belmont, "Big Billie" took over the Mikado. In June 1939, she found herself in trouble with the law, not for running a whorehouse, but for killing three buck sheep near Howardsville. The San Juan County Historical Society has a summary of a court trial made by one of the jurors. The report stated that the sheep were killed about October 10, 1938, by Fred Markel, ("Big Billie's" pimp) and John Anzig. (probably Anzek, Frances' husband) The prosecuting attorney claimed that Betty Wagner, ("Big Billie") encouraged the men to kill the sheep. One of the witnesses in the case was Ruby Hiar. She testified that in October she worked for Betty Wagner at the Mikado "a beer parlor and whorehouse here in town." The writer of the report commented in parentheses that "this trial was especially juicy as it was nothing but a whorehouse brawl. If this should SHOCK you, don't read any more." The trial lasted from Thursday until 10 a. m. Sunday morning. The jury was hung with seven voting guilty and five for acquittal. To quote the juror "We all agreed in our own minds the defendants were guilty but it all boiled down to the point whether the State had proved them guilty beyond a reasonable doubt in our minds. Did the State have sufficient evidence to back up the testimony of the accomplices? Did they prove that they were at the scene of the crime when the crime was committed? Did they connect the Mikado with the crime?"

Many of the prostitutes in Silverton ended up in the Mikado. It was one of the last bordellos to operate before Blair Street was cleaned up.

OLLIE KELLY

Ollie Kelly was a woman of the "line" who had worked at the National Hall before coming to the Mikado. Ollie had a son in Kansas to whom she regularly sent money. Nona Salfisberg befriended Ollie in the mid-1930's. Ollie would wait until Nona left her home to work in her beauty shop. When the house was empty, Ollie would come in and wash all the dishes and clean the house thoroughly. In return, Nona, and her first husband, Joe Vota, would feed her. Ollie worked at the Mikado for several years.

"BABE" OR "BLONDE PEGGY"

"Babe" or "Blonde Peggy" as she was often called, worked for "Jew" Fanny at the National Hall for a while. She later moved to the Mikado where she worked for several years. She eventually married one of the local boys.

The Mikado operated into the 1940's. On February 7, 1949, Fred Markel, mentioned above, received a tax deed to the property for 1934 back taxes. The tax sale was actually in December of 1935, but the deed was not issued until fourteen years later, in 1949. He paid the $137.73 back taxes for the property. On July 14, 1952, Fred Markel sold the Mikado to Nick Bonaventura. Bonaventura used the building to store bakery equipment. The building was destroyed by fire in 1954 while under Bonaventura's ownership.

THE MIKADO

A new two story frame building known as the Lookout was built on the lot in the late 1980's.

Fig. 71 The Lookout Building occupies the site of the Mikado Saloon. 1992 Allan Bird Photo.

---

26   The Mikado was located on the west side of Blair Street, three lots north of 12th Street.

27   The Benson Building is the large brick structure directly across the street from the Grand Imperial Hotel.

CHAPTER TWENTY-THREE
THE
BELLVIEW SALOON
AND BOARDING HOUSE

Presently Zhivago's Restaurant

Fig. 72 1954 photo of the old Bellview Saloon. Signs were for movie set. Ruth Gregory Collection.

The Bellview Saloon was built on the site of Riley Lambert's Dance Hall, one of Silverton's earliest bordellos. The building was next door, to the south, from Tom Cain's Dance Hall. Robert Roberts sold the lot to Lambert in November 1882 for $400. Lambert built the dance hall that year. In 1883, Lambert was killed by Marshal Tom Cain. The building was allowed to deteriorate over the years. In 1888, the estate of Riley Lambert sold the property to W. D. Pascoe, the town doctor. In 1890, the building was gone and the land assessed at $62.

Fig. 73 East Side of Blair Street looking from 13th toward 11th Street, about 1948. Bellview Saloon at left of photo. Andy Hanahan Photo.

LOUIS SARTORE

On March 17, 1893, Dr. Pascoe sold the lot to Louis Sartore for $100. Sartore built a small structure and the assessment was doubled to $200 in 1896. In 1897, Louis Sartore moved a small structure onto the lot next door, to the south, and used it as a saloon and cigar store. In 1899, Louis Sartore built the Bellview Saloon, which still stands.

On March 17, 1901, Louis Sartore died. He was born in Piemonte Province, Italy, on February 25, 1853. He had lived in Silverton since 1878. Between 1878 and 1892, he worked as a miner. In 1892 he went into the saloon business. His main saloon was located where the north half of the Teller House now stands on Greene Street. In 1897, he moved to Blair Street. The cause of his death was gangrene of the lung, brought on by a bout of pneumonia. He left a wife, two daughters, and a son Philip, who later took over the Bellview Saloon.

JOHN GIONO

Mrs. Sartore continued to run the saloon and upstairs boarding house until 1906, when the building was leased to John Giono. The lease was to run from July 1, 1905, until July 1, 1915. Rent was to be $70 per month. Giono ran the saloon until December 1910, when Louis' son, Philip Sartore, took over the saloon and boarding house. John Giono moved across the street and built the Piemonte Saloon and Boarding House.[28] During Prohibition, Philip Sartore operated a still in the basement of the Bellview. He made his own whiskey and Zinfandel wine. Several times he was "busted" by the Federal agents. The sink in the bar had iron bars across it so that bottles could be quickly smashed in case of a raid. "They couldn't arrest you for smelling it" was Sartore's comment. After each raid, he would make a new batch. During those times, the saloon fronted as a pool hall. Mrs. Sartore maintained the family residence in a portion of the upstairs over the saloon. In the remaining area she ran a boarding house for miners. She charged $1 a day for room and board. Drinks in the saloon were 25 cents for whiskey and two-for-a-quarter for beer. Philip Sartore ran the Bellview for thirty-eight years until May 13, 1948, when he sold the property to John Paul Troglia.

Fig. 74 Jess Carey in the Bellview Saloon. He operated a museum in the building in the late 1950's. San Juan Co. Hist. Soc. Photo.

THE BELLVIEW SALOON & BOARDING HOUSE

The Bellview was never a bordello. During the 1950's, Jess Carey ran a museum in the building. In 1955, it was used as a set in the movie "Great Day In The Morning" when it was named the Free State Saloon. Since the early 1970's, the building has housed Zhivago's Restaurant.

Fig. 75 Present-day Bellview Saloon, now Zhivago's Restaurant. May, 1986. Allan Bird Photo.

---

[28] The Piemonte Saloon and Boarding House occupied the southwest corner of 13th and Blair Streets. Gionos owned the two corner lots north of Swanee's Gift Shop.

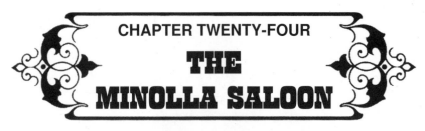

CHAPTER TWENTY-FOUR
THE
MINOLLA SALOON

Presently Swanee's Gift Shop.

The first building on the lot was a small crib built in 1893 by G. A. Ambold, a local butcher. The building, like most cribs, was assessed at $50. On September 6, 1898, Lottie Ambold, Administratrix to Ambold's estate, sold the property to F. H. Hinderer for $200. Hinderer leased out the crib for a few years. On March 30, 1901, he sold the property to Domenica Dalla and Modestto Todeschi for $325. Domenica received a one-third interest and Todeschi a two-thirds interest. In 1902, they erected the present stone building, which is now occupied by Swanee's Gift Shop.[29] The building was built by unemployed Tyrolean stone masons from rock quarried near the mouth of Cement Creek, to the north of town.

JOHN DALLA

Shortly after completion of the building, John Dalla, whose full name was Dallavalle, opened the Tyrolean Saloon. John died from the after-effects of severe frostbite which he received while driving cattle to Silverton over Molas Pass during the winter months. Domencia, John's wife, had eleven children. She ran a boarding house located on the east bank of Cement Creek.

MINOLLA

After John Dalla's death in 1911, the property was leased to a man by the name of Minolla. The time frame within which Minolla operated his saloon is not definitely known. Probably until local Prohibition in 1916. After Minolla left, the building was rented out for rooms from time to time. Several people tried to operate a small bar along with the rooming house.

During the flu epidemic of 1918, Domenica Dalla, along with two of her sons died on the same day. Mary Dalla was orphaned at the age of sixteen with three small brothers, Fury, age 11, Louis, age 10 and Herman, age 6. Mary ran her mother's boarding house and supported herself and three brothers. Mary related how her mother worked so hard caring for her family and her boarding house, that she never got downtown to Greene Street, a distance of three blocks, for nine years.

Fig. 76 Minolla's Saloon, originally John Dalla's Tyrolian Saloon. 1954 photo shows old Swanson's Market. Porch was built for a movie set. Ruth Gregory Collection.

SWANSON'S MARKET

The saloon property on Blair Street was left to Mary Dalla Swanson and her older brother Joe. Joe was an engineer on the D. & R. G. Railroad at Alamosa. He gave his share of the building to Mary. In 1941, she opened Swanson's Market. When she received the building there was a tax lien against the property. She did not have enough money to pay off the taxes. She had a small insurance policy which she was able to borrow against and pay off the back taxes. She repaid this loan at the rate of $5 per month. She had something like $25 or $35 left, with which she started Swanson's Market. She raised her family upstairs above the store. The store prospered and Mary retired a few years ago and has since passed on. Since 1990, her son Gerald and his daughters now operate the store as Swanee's Gift Shop.

The building was never a bordello.

Fig. 77 Old Tryrolian Saloon, later Minolla's Saloon, followed by Swanson's Market-Now Swanee's Gift Shop. 1992 Allan Bird Photo.

---

[29] The Minolla Saloon occupied the present Swanee's Gift Shop Building on west side of Blair Street, three lots south of 13th Street.

CHAPTER TWENTY-FIVE
THE
PIEMONTE SALOON
& BOARDING HOUSE

Fig. 78 John Giono's Piemonte Saloon and Boarding House—1917. John Giono in white shirt. John Anzek, later Frances Belmont's husband, in doorway. The three Palmer Brothers in front of building. One of the Palmer Brothers died in the flu epidemic of 1918. Jim Bell Collection.

John Giono's (pronounced Guy-no) Piemonte Saloon and Boarding House was built on the site of Mary Scheidt's home, one of Silverton's oldest residences.[30] Mary Scheidt's house was set back from the front of the lot. On February 19, 1906, she leased the front fifty feet of the lot fronting Blair Street to local blacksmiths, C. S. Casad and Ben Cain, for $75 per year with the provision that "they could erect any building they so desired. They must abide by the law."

171

JOHN GIONO

On July 21, 1910, Mary Scheidt sold the property to Caterina Giono for $1400. Her husband, John Giono, had been leasing Sartore's Bellview Saloon, across the street, since 1905. When the Gionos took over the property, there were three buildings on the two lots, one was a blacksmith shop. They tore down the existing buildings and built a large boarding house and saloon, filling the entire one hundred feet of the corner lot. They built a small lean-to kitchen on the lot to the south which adjoined the large building. The saloon had a corner entrance and was a popular place with the miners. The boarding house catered to miners only. The Gionos operated the Piemonte until John Giono's death in 1932.

According to Jim Hook, Sr., the saloon was taken over by Martin Cina and his brother Paco:

> The place was a bootleg joint with girls. Paco died and left Martin with the business. When he was there by himself the girls would get Martin so drunk he would pass out. The girls would put him to bed and then have a party using Martin's liquor. This cost him money. They gave away all his booze.

It is not known how long Martin Cina operated the property or who followed him but it did remain in the Giono family.

In November of 1944, Lydia Giono McCarrier quit-claimed lot 23, the lot adjacent to Swanson's Market, to Mary Swanson for $1. In 1944, a man by the name of Hayes, from Cortez, Colorado, bought the Piemonte Saloon and Boarding House for back taxes. He demolished the building for the lumber. The property was transferred to Tom Hadden. Hadden gave the land to Mary Swanson for filling in the hole left by the old basement. Mary paid $600 to have enough dirt hauled to reclaim the land. Both corner lots are now owned by the Swansons.

THE PIEMONTE SALOON & BOARDING HOUSE

The Piemonte was never a bordello during the time that the Gionos operated the property. After 1932, when the Cinas operated the saloon, it was a bordello.

Fig. 79 John Giono—1863-1932. He died in Durango during one of Silverton's lengthy snow blockades. It was over a month before his body could be returned to Silverton for burial. Photo taken from his gravestone—Damaged by vandals. Allan Bird Photo.

Fig. 80 Former location of the Piemonte Saloon and Boarding House. Southwest corner of 13th and Blair streets. Old Swanson Market at left. 1986 Allan Bird Photo.

---

[30] Mary Scheidt's house was located on the southwest corner of 13th and Blair streets.

CHAPTER TWENTY-SIX
THE ARCADE

Fig 81   Photo of Arcade Recreation Hall, about 1939. The Diamond Belle is to the left of the photo. Jim Bell Collection.

The Arcade Saloon was the last saloon built on Blair Street. It is located on the northeast corner of 12th and Blair. (beside the train stop) This building was constructed in 1929, during the Prohibition era. Officially it was the Arcade Recreation Hall. They served bootleg whiskey and kept several women in the back rooms. It was not Silverton's first Arcade Saloon. There was an Arcade about the turn of the century that was located at the site of the old Goode's Saloon on Greene Street. For years, the two corner lots,[31] contained two and later three cribs. One of the oldest cribs was built on the lot next door to the Arcade by Francis Rawley in 1882. The first building to be constructed on the corner lot was probably built in 1905 by C. A. Leonard, one of Silverton's law officers.

Leonard acquired the property from Orrin Bosworth on November 8, 1905. The transaction included "a warranty deed on lots 11 and 12, block 19, for $1 plus furniture, carpets, stoves, books, Does not apply to 1/2 interest in lot 12." It is not known who owned the other half-interest in lot 12, the future site of the Arcade.

During Leonard's ownership, which lasted until 1920, a third crib was built on the property line between lots 11 and 12. These cribs were occupied by some of the more colorful women of Blair Street.

"BLACK MINNIE" HEBERLINE

For a time, the corner crib was occupied by "Black Minnie" Heberline. She later married Philip Sartore, the owner of the Bellview Saloon. "Black" Minnie was not black in color but in disposition. She derived the nickname by being vicious with any woman that dared to take away her customers. After Phil and Minnie Sartore sold the Bellview Saloon in 1948, they moved to Durango where Phil worked as a bartender in the Elk's Club until he retired.

For a short period of time, Sadie Walker, another "Soiled Dove," occupied the corner crib.

The original crib, built by Frances Rawley on lot 11 was sold to Fred Sherwin in 1885. Sherwin was the local dry goods merchant who, in 1880, built the stone building on the corner of 13th and Greene streets.[32] He leased the crib out to prostitutes. By 1892, the taxes were assessed to Peter Houghton, Sherwin's partner in the dry goods business. On February 23, 1894, Peter Houghton sold the lot and crib to Jack Smith for $200 "plus improvements." Smith was in partnership with a person named Duerr. It is possible that Duerr was a prostitute. The following year the property was listed under Jack and Emma Smith. Perhaps Jack Smith married Emma Duerr, however, this is pure speculation. Smith made news in January 1900, when his crib was raided as a suspected opium joint. The January 20, 1900, edition of the *Silverton Standard* printed the following story:

Last Tuesday night Marshal Lyle and Nightwatch Leonard raided a few "hop" joints and took in the inmates who were 'hitting the pipe.' The following almond-eyed heathens were gobbled up by the officers: Joe, Dutch, Wang and Tom, who gave bond to appear before Squire Watsons the following day. The places raided are located over the Saddle Rock Restaurant, and Jack Smith's place opposite Ludwig's Dance Hall on Blair Street. No one was found in the latter dive. Four fined $8.70 to $37.70. These dens of iniquity should be raided at every opportunity as it is a rotten spot on the character of a city the size of Silverton to be infected with such hell holes.

On March 23, 1903, Jack Smith sold lot 11 and 1/2 interest in lot 12 to Orrin Bosworth. Bosworth, as mentioned above, sold the properties to Leonard. On April 17, 1920, Leonard sold the two lots, in which he was now the full owner, to Barney Tocco. Tocco leased out the cribs until August 1927, when he sold the two properties to Sam Manick for $350. Sam Manick sold the lots, on November 16, 1929, to Glenn Edwards and Jim Sparlin for $4400. This would indicate that Sam Manick was the man who built the Arcade in early 1929.

Corky Scheer recalls that they sold bootleg whiskey in the Arcade. For a short period of time, probably sometime between 1929 and 1933, "Big Billie" worked out of the Arcade. He recalls throwing a rock at her as she stood in front of the building. He missed and broke the window.

On June 7, 1932, Glenn Edwards and Jim Sparlin sold the Arcade and the adjacent lot to Luigia Mattivi for $4400, "including all furniture

Fig. 82. 1954 photo of the Arcade. Cafe sign may have been for movie set. Ruth Gregory Collection.

and fixtures." By 1946, the building and lots were owned by Marselino Gallegos.

The building looks much the same today as it did when it was first built. For years it has sported the orange coat of paint. Today it is a curio shop for tourists.

Fig. 83 Arcade Gift Shop, Summer of 1986. Allan Bird Photo.

---

[31] Before the Arcade was built, the two lots on the northeast corner of 12th and Blair contained three small cribs.

[32] This building is now occupied by the Pickle Barrel Restaurant.

CHAPTER TWENTY-SEVEN
THE
NORTH POLE SALOON

Fig. 84 1914 photo showing the North Pole Saloon and Boarding House. *Eddie Lorenzon Photo.*

The North Pole Saloon is the only large saloon that was north of 13th Street. The building still stands on the west side of Blair Street, four lots north of 13th.

As early as 1896, Angelo Todeschi was assessed $50 for a small building, possibly a crib, on lot 16, block 13. In January 1900, Anibele Marli sold the property to Georgio Baldessari for $300 "plus all improvements." On March 14, 1901, Baldessari sold the land to Matt Chiono for $100. This was for land only, no buildings were on the property at this time. Matt Chiono had been a partner with Louis Giacomelli in the Iron Mountain Saloon on the corner of 13th and Greene streets. This was in the original Sherwin and

THE NORTH POLE SALOON

Fig. 85 Two Men with "snowshoes" in front of the North Pole Saloon, about 1920. Andy Hanahan Photo.

Houghton building, now the Pickle Barrel. The faded "Iron Mountain Saloon" sign can still be seen on the side of the building.

On May 3, 1902, Matt Chiono began building the two-story frame building, which was to become the North Pole Saloon. The building served as a saloon and boarding house. It was completed in early June 1902. The original building was 24 X 60 feet in size. Later in 1904, an additional forty feet was added to the rear of the structure, thus covering the entire 100 feet of the lot. It is not known how long the Chiono family operated the North Pole. During an interview with Annie Smith and Corky Scheer about their memories of Blair Street, Corky recalled that "in the late 1930's, some guys from Chicago had the North Pole. They had three girls from Arizona working there." Annie Smith interrupted with "the North Pole was never a hook-shop." Corky's reply was. "The hell it wasn't, I was there." According to Corky, "Bogolini had the North Pole after the two guys from Denver in the 1940's."

During the time that the North Pole was operated by the Chiono family, it was used as a saloon and boarding house for miners. It was not a bor-

Fig. 86 1954 photo of the North Pole Saloon, leaning dangerously to the right. Ruth Gregory Collection.

dello. This is one of those buildings whose use depended upon the current operator.

Hollywood used the interior of the North Pole Saloon for a set in the movie "Night Passage," filmed in 1957 with Jimmy Stewart and Audie Murphy.

In the mid-1970's, the building was leaning precariously toward the north. Today the building has been propped up and covered with plywood. It is currently being used as a carpenter shop.

Fig. 87 The North Pole Saloon, semi-restored, 1986.
Allan Bird Photo.

CHAPTER TWENTY-EIGHT
THE CRIBS
& THE GIRLS

Blair Street was lined with a mixture of large bordellos, saloons, and boarding houses, separated by numerous small cribs. Many of these cribs were later replaced with large buildings which have been discussed in previous chapters. To avoid duplication, these cribs will not be mentioned in this chapter.

Many of Silverton's more colorful "independent" prostitutes operated out of their own cribs. Perhaps the three most famous during the thirty years prior to World War II were Lola Daggett, whose trade name was "Nigger" Lola, "Diamond Tooth" Leona, whose real name was Leona Wallace, and Fanny Wright, whose alias was "Jew" Fanny. In addition to these ladies were others who operated cribs: Pearl Eastman, "Tar Baby" Brown, Mayme Murphy, Rose Lane, to name only four.

Fig. 88 Photo of "Nigger" Lola when she was young. About 1910. Andy Hanahan Photo.

"NIGGER" LOLA'S

Presently the Emporium Gift Shop.

The house, which was later purchased by Lola Daggett, was built by E. L. Roberts in 1896. The building was a four-room structure, located two doors south of the Bon Ton on the west side of Blair Street between 11th and 12th streets. The house first made news in September 1898, when it was occupied by a prostitute whose name was Laura Leighton. The _Silverton Standard_ printed the following story:

181

CHAPTER TWENTY-EIGHT

Laura is derived from the word laurel, which means green. Sweet Laura Leighton, however, who for a year past, occupied one of E. L. Robert's seaside cottages on Blair Street, last week put the kibosh on the green part of her name and proved up that she was dead ripe in the ways of the wicked. The lady, who had many admirers on account of her virtue and other adornments, suddenly disappeared from their view and slid, it is supposed, into New Mexico. Mr. Roberts felt rather lopsided on the deal as Laura owed him $138 for a parlor set which she had taken the precaution to dispose of prior to her leaving. It is supposed that the furniture is in town although at this writing no trace of it has been discovered. The woman owed Prosser also for a carpet. Mr. Roberts has telegraphed to Laura's reputed new stamping ground in New Mexico, but we believe the gentle ticker failed to find her.

In July 1905, Roberts sold the building to C. C. Koennecker for $500.

Lola Daggett was born in northern Colorado and was raised in Pueblo. She arrived in Silverton about 1904. John Matties, who was born in 1909, remembers Lola when he was a small boy. Lola

Fig. 89 1914 photo showing crib that later became "Nigger" Lola's house. West side of Blair Street between 11th and 12th streets. Photo also shows Lola's second bordello. Eddie Lorenzon Photo.

had a sister named Freda. Freda was a mulatto and the two of them operated their crib as partners. According to John, when he was only three years old, he was told by his mother and father that Freda was half white. Years later his parents told him that he was always trying to peek in their doorway trying to see which half of her was white. Freda died in 1912 at the age of 35.

Lola was a rather tall, plumpish black woman. It is not known where Lola lived and worked during her early years in Silverton. On November 20, 1922, she bought C. C. Koennecker's four-room house at 1135 Blair Street. She operated out of this house for several years, usually with one or two girls working with her.

During the late 1920's, Lola moved three doors up the street to a small house adjacent to the Matties' Boarding House. This house was built by Albert Mayers in 1896 and sold to Louisa Crawford the same year. The house was owned by Mary Kloster from 1901 until 1945. It was rented out as a crib. Emma Wilson was one of the inmates during the early 1920's. Lola rented her original house to girls on the "line" as a crib. The new building was much larger. She needed the space for her expanded business. Lola kept several black girls working in her new crib. She always had a black woman piano player to provide entertainment. According to those who knew her, she kept a "clean" house and was well patronized by the local businessmen. One attorney in town was strongly fascinated by Lola. He was married and had a family, but each night he would sneak down the alley, thinking he was unobserved, to visit her. "Jew" Fanny, whose window faced Lola's alley, reported to Nona Salfisberg that "she seen ____ going to Lola's almost every night." Lola had the reputation of being the "businessman's girl friend" in Silverton. Jim Bell related the story of how one of her customers had asked her "if that black ever rubbed off." She told him that "there wouldn't be a businessman in Silverton that would dare go home if it did."

During the late 1920's Lola prospered. She always wore an expensive fur coat downtown when she went for her mail. Julia Maffey recalled meeting her in the post office one day and commenting on her beautiful fur coat. Lola told her that "she could have one too if she was in the right business."

In her way, Lola was able to counteract the crude way in which blacks were treated during this period of time. She had a "white" chauffeur. His name was Bud Martin and he also served as her pimp. Martin operated a restaurant located on the corner of 12th and Blair streets, a short distance from Lola's crib. In 1927, Lola was assessed $990 for a 1927 Buick Sedan. She always had the finest of cars even though she could not drive. She worked as a Madame and kept several girls working until her health failed in 1937.

Fig. 90 "Nigger" Lola Daggett (standing) with one of her "girls" outside her last bordello. Matties' Boarding House at right. About 1935. San Juan Co. Hist. Soc. Photo.

After she became sick, Rosa Stewart, the owner of the Avon Hotel took her in and cared for her. Rosa's Avon was not a bordello; however, many of the women of the "line" would go there for their "coffee breaks." The Avon is on the corner of 10th and Blair, therefore, unlike Greene Street, there were no restrictions on the women's movements.

Fig. 91 Rosa Stewart's Avon Hotel being gutted by fire in 1938. Rosa took care of Lola when Lola was dying. Northwest corner of 10th and Blair Streets. Tom Savich Photo.

THE CRIBS & THE GIRLS

Lola was well liked in Silverton. She was especially kind to the small children who frequently ran errands and chopped wood for her. She was an excellent cook. According to John Matties, Lola made "the best candy you ever tasted." The kids would go to her back door and she always had homemade candy for them.

Lola died on November 26, 1939. A synopsis of her last will and testament read as follows:

> I, Lola Daggett, have no known relatives living. I wish to leave my insurance policy for $300 plus my four-room house at 1135 Blair Street, Lot 18, Block 29, plus money or possessions I may own at the time of my death to my friend, Rosa Stewart.

Lola was listed as being 50 years old in her obituary. John and Joe Matties said she was much older; "Lola always lied about her age."

The present Emporium Gift Shop occupies Lola's original home.

Fig. 92 Avon Hotel about 1950. The hotel was built in 1904 by F. O. Sherwood. It was used as a meat market and rooming house. Jim Bell Collection.

Fig. 93 Lola's first house on Blair Street, now occupied by the Emporium Gift Shop. 1992 Allan Bird Photo.

185

"DIAMOND TOOTH" LEONA

Lot North of Zhivago's Restaurant

Leona Wallace, known as "Diamond Tooth" Leona because of the diamond she had set in her front tooth, came to Silverton about 1923, after the closure of the whorehouses in Telluride. Several of the more famous women of the "line" arrived at this time. "Jew" Fanny and "Big Billie" were two who were forced to leave Telluride with Leona. According to Corky Scheer, "Diamond Tooth" Leona "wasn't too good looking a gal." Julia Maffey, whose father owned the French Bakery remembers Leona as working out of the Tree Top, next to the Laundry, when she first arrived in Silverton. Later, Leona moved into the building that had been Maffey's French Bakery, on the site of Tom Cain's old dance hall. On December 21, 1918, near the end of the flu epidemic, Machetto and Maffey sold the building to Joe Chiono. Chiono, and his wife Mary, leased the building to the girls of the "line." "Diamond Tooth" Leona probably rented the building about 1925 from the Chionos. She became a Madame and had several girls working for her. The San Juan County Historical Society has a copy of her December, 1928 telephone bill. All of the calls were to various bordellos in Leadville, Telluride and Durango.

"Leach" Zanoni told the story of how Leona tried to kill Corky Scheer. It was during the winter and he managed somehow to really irritate her. She reached in her drawer and pulled out a large revolver. The snow was piled about six feet deep along the middle of Blair Street. Corky ran out and jumped over the snow bank. As he ran down the street, she chased him with only the snow bank separating the two. When she got a glimpse of him she would fire over the top of the bank, fortunatly for Corky, she was a poor shot.

In December 1929, Mary Chiono sold the property to Yettie Unfussing for $2000. "Diamond Tooth" Leona continued to lease the property from Yettie until January of 1938 when she sold it to "Black Minnie" Sartore. According to Nona Salfisberg, "Diamond Tooth" Leona continued to work out of this house until "about

1940." Nona moved to Silverton in 1933 and did Leona's hair. Shortly before the War, Leona and "her man" moved to Albuquerque, New Mexico where they bought a motel and lived a respectable life.

According to Gerald Swanson, owner of Swanee's Gift Shop across the street, the building burned to the ground in 1940.

Fig. 94 Dorothy "Tar Baby" Brown. About 1907. Note the sad eyes. She died in 1971. Fritz Klinke Photo.

DOROTHY "TAR BABY" BROWN

"Tar Baby" Brown was a mulatto. She came to Silverton as a teenager about the same time as "Nigger" Lola, probably around 1905. She was born in Chicago, Illinois, on May 1, 1889, and was raised in an orphanage. "Tar Baby" worked, for the most part, out of cribs. For a while, she worked out of one of the cribs on the corner later occupied by the Arcade Saloon. She once told Corky Scheer of how she had spent time in the old 1883 wooden jail, now located on Greene Street. Her life must have been extremely hard, since she had been raised as an unwanted child in a Chicago orphanage. She later entered the life of prostitution as a teenager in Silverton. She had a son who was killed in an accident in 1954. The general comment made by all who knew her was that she was one of the toughest gals on the "line." She would fight with the other women, and often with her customers.

Dorothy married Frank Brown, a Silverton native. The late Eddie Lorenzon told of knowing Frank and "Tar Baby":

> Brown was the sheriff or marshal for a long time. He drank quite heavily, but was big enough to hold his liquor. After they were married, they moved into a house near the south edge of town. It was a 'pig pen.' She would roll her own cigarettes and after she had smoked them down to the butts, she would flick them against the ceiling and walls, where they would stick. Her whole house was covered with old cigarette butts. She had her own crib on Blair Street and was one of the rougher women on the "row." She was almost black, that's why they called her "Tar Baby." She was very old when she died.

Dorothy Brown lived to the ripe old age of 82 years. She died in Durango on February 2, 1971. She is buried in Hillside Cemetery, Silverton, Colorado.

Fig. 95 Mayme Murphy's Crib, also used by "Jew" Fanny for a short time. "Green" House at left, Rose Lane's Crib at right. About 1949. Jim Bell Collection.

MAYME MURPHY

Mayme Murphy, like most of the others, moved several times during her sojourn on Blair Street. In 1900, Ludwig Vota built a small crib on the lot directly south of the "Green House" on the east side of Blair Street, between 11th and 12th streets. Dozens of prostitutes occupied this crib over the years; however, only two are remembered; Mayme Murphy and "Jew" Fanny. John and Joe Matties, who lived across the street, remembered Mayme Murphy living in that "small house." "She was older." Mary Swanson remembers her as "an old ornery old lady on the 'line' who would curse at the kids." Mayme was stricken with a bout of aching muscles. One night she plugged in her heating pad and electrocuted herself in her small crib.

After Mayme's death, "Jew" Fanny worked out of this crib for a short time.

The building was destroyed in the January 16, 1968, fire that destroyed Fattor's Tremount Saloon and Rose Lane's crib.

ROSE LANE

Rose Lane origi-
nally worked out of
the old Stone Saloon
building, next to
Swanee's Gift Shop.
She later moved and
was one of the last
prostitutes to occupy
the small crib di-
rectly next door to
the south, of Mayme
Murphy's crib. This
crib was also built
by Ludwig Vota, in
1897. Rose Lane
married Carl Blake,
a mine blacksmith.
Mary Swanson's

Fig. 96 Rose Lane's Crib, later occupied by Dr. Holt.
January 16, 1968 fire, which destroyed much of the
block, started in this building. 1954 photo. Sign
used for movie set. Ruth Gregory Collection.

comment was that, "Carl Blake's wife was an ornery old devil.
Thought she was the queen of Silverton—She came off the 'line'."
Jim Hook, Sr. remembered Rose as "Big Freda." He said that "after
Silverton closed down it's red light district, "Big Freda" and Carl
were married. They bought a ranch in Oklahoma and retired. Carl
died on Stony Pass, while visiting Silverton. 'Freda' was long and
tall, of Alsace-Lorraine extraction."

After Rose Lane moved from the crib, it was occupied by Dr. Holt,
one of the town's doctors. Dr. Holt had a drinking problem. On
January 16, 1968, fire broke out in Dr. Holt's home which resulted in
the destruction of both of Ludwig Vota's old cribs and Fattor's
Tremount Saloon, which was, at the time of the fire, being occupied
by the first Bent Elbow Restaurant. It is thought that Dr. Holt's
drinking may have contributed to carelessness which caused the fire.

Fig. 97 1954 photo showing the Green Lantern, a small Blair Street Bordello. Tremount Saloon on left and Zanoni-Pedroni's Florence Saloon on right. Ruth Gregory Collection.

THE GREEN LANTERN

A small wooden house was built on lot 8, next door, to the south of Fattor's Tremont Saloon. The structure was built by Shephard and Wheeler in 1896 and served as a crib. The house was used as a residence by Celeste and "Big Tillie" Fattor during Tillie's lifetime. Jim Hook, Sr. recalls that it was called the "Green Lantern" during the 1920's. Little is known of this structure. The property changed hands frequently over the years. In 1933, a sheriff's deed was issued to Mrs. Sam Eccher, the owner of the Tremount Liquor Store next door. It was probably torn down in the late 1950's.

SMALL CRIB

This building was next door to the north of the present Silverton Candle and Gift Shop, owned by Ruth Ward. The crib was built by William Murry in 1897. In 1902, Jack Matties purchased the crib for rental purposes. After Jack Matties' death in 1903, the property reverted back to William Murry. Murry also owned the adjacent lot to the south, lot 5. On October 10, 1906, he sold both lots and the included buildings to Peter Orella for $1000. Caterina Giono bought the two lots from Orella in 1910. She, in turn, sold them to Barney Tocco in October 1916 for $1,000. The original crib has long since been demolished. Tocco converted the crib next door, to the south, into his Piemonte Grocery and Shoe Store.

Fig. 98 1954 photo showing Louis Satore's Crib on right. Painted for a movie set. Ruth Gregory Collection.

LOUIS SARTORE'S CRIB

Next door, to the south of Barney Tocco's store, was a small wooden crib at 1240 Blair Street which today is part of the Hitching Post. This building was constructed in 1897 by J. H. Faught. That same year, Faught sold the ground to Ottis Ballou, an early day Silverton merchant, for $200. Shortly after Ballou obtained the land, probably for an unpaid bill, he deeded the property to the Gold King Mining and Milling Company for use as an office.

In August 1900, Gold King sold the crib to Louis Sartore. During Sartore's ownership, he leased it out to prostitutes. Minnie Davis and Josie Alexander both worked out of 1240 Blair Street. In 1947, Philip Sartore, Louis Sartore's son, sold the property to Jess Carey. In 1950, he sold it to Rosa Stewart, owner of the Avon Hotel.

SMALL CRIB

At least three separate buildings occupied this ground at different times over the years. This lot is directly to the north of the Diamond Belle on the east side of Blair Street, between 12th and 13th streets.

As early as 1881, Joe Wallace was assessed $100 for a building on lot 9. By 1900, the vacant lot was owned by E. L. Roberts. In 1901, Roberts built a large structure which was assessed $900 by the county. This was undoubtedly a bordello. Between 1900 and 1904, the building probably burned down. The 1904 assessment for building was $0.

On May 15, 1905, Emma Roberts, E. L. Roberts' wife, sold the land with a small building to Louisa Maurell, the owner of the Diamond Belle next door, for $425. That same day, Louisa sold it to Peter Orella for $500. In November 1909, Orella sold the crib to John Mattivi, owner of the Monte Carlo, two doors to the north, for $500. In July of 1913, Mattivi sold the crib to Pasquale Cina for $500. Cina owned the crib until September 1929, when he deeded it to Constanza Orella. The exact date of the building's demise is not known. There appears to be some real question about the existence of buildings on this lot after the Mattivi's purchased it in 1909. Eddie Lorenzon's 1914 photograph of Blair Street shows a vacant lot south of the Diamond Belle. John Matties remembers only a vacant lot during his lifetime.

Fig. 99 Todeschi's Stone Saloon, built in 1897.   1990 Allan Bird Photo.

THE STONE SALOON CRIB

The Stone Saloon, next door to the south of Swanee's Gift Shop, was built in 1897 by Joe Todeschi. Joe Todeschi had borrowed money on the building and could not repay his debt. In July 1901 the property was sold to Jack Matties at a sheriff's sale. Matties, on that same day, sold the saloon back to Modesto Todeschi and Domenica Dallavalle for the $1528.33 judgment against the property. Domenica owned 1/3 of the property and the

THE CRIBS & THE GIRLS

Todeschi Brothers owned the remaining 2/3's. The Todeschi's and Dallavalle's were related. About a year later, the July 26, 1902, *Silverton Standard* printed the following story about the Stone Saloon:

> No less that three attempts have been made within the past ten days to injure some of the occupants of the stone building on Blair Street next door to the Tyrolean Saloon. The first trouble occurred Friday night of last week, when some miscreant threw a large rock through a window, which narrowly missed a woman and wrecked a stove. Sunday night another stone was thrown against the window, but no damage was done further than smashing several panes of glass. Wednesday George Innes, a well-known miner, was arrested on suspicion of being the miscreant, but as there was no evidence to hold him he was dismissed. That same night, for a third time, a rock was hurled against the window and a third time it was broken. There is absolutely no clue to the guilty person.

The building was a saloon and small crib from the time it was built. Peter Dalla was shot in this saloon in 1904. The ownership in later years is not known. Several women rented the building as a crib in the 1920's and later. Among the inhabitants of this crib were "Black Minnie" Heberline, (Philip Sartore's future wife) and Rose Lane, (Carl Blake's future wife.)

Fig. 100 Blow up of west side of Blair Street from 1914 panarama photo showing Louis Satore's and Pearl Eastman's cribs. Eddie Lorenzon Photo.

PEARL EASTMAN

(Please see photo on preceding page)

This crib was located two doors south of the old 1883 Silverton City Hall, on the west side of Blair Street between 12th and 13th streets. In 1899, F. H. Hinderer built the small building as a crib. In February 1907, he sold it to Nellie Stafford for $800. Nellie was probably a girl of the "line." A year later, she sold the crib to Joe Corazza, owner of the National Hall, for $850.

Some time prior to 1918, Corazza leased the crib to Pearl Eastman. Pearl was a prostitute who later supposedly married George Sitter. Many of the prostitutes would say that they were married to their pimps for appearance sake. George was a cook by trade. The late Jim Cole, Sr. related the story of how George was determined to save some money, which he entrusted to Pearl. When he asked her for his savings, she told him that she had gambled it all away. He was furious and picked her up and threw her out the window, "sash and all." After he recovered from his initial outburst of temper, he realized that was a "damn fool thing to do." He went out and carried her back in. He knew the only hope he had of getting his money back was to put her to work and earn it.

Pearl was one of the prostitutes who acted as a nurse during the flu epidemic of 1918. She contracted the disease and paid with her life. She is buried in an unmarked grave in Hillside Cemetery at Silverton.

The ownership of the crib remained with the Corazza family until the 1930's. It was probably torn down in the late 1930's or early 1940's.

The building stood on the present site of the Chamber of Commerce "Potty" Park.

THEODORE DICK'S CRIB

In 1883, Theodore Dick built one of the early cribs on the southwest corner of Blair and 12th streets, next door, to the north of Matties' Welcome Saloon. Some time before the turn of the century, he added two more buildings facing 12th Street to the lot. One was a small cabin adjoining the alley which "Denver" Kate rented in her old age. The center building was a Chinese restaurant until 1902, when the Chinese were driven from Silverton. After the Chinese left, the building remained empty until it was destroyed by vandals. The old house on the corner was leased as a crib until March 1907, when Theodore Dick sold the property to Billy Luke for $2500.

Luke operated the dance hall across the street, to the north. Over the years, Luke rented the crib to various prostitutes. For awhile the corner house was the "Hot Tomale Place," one of Silverton's first Mexican restaurants. Later it was operated as a restaurant by Bud Martin, "Nigger" Lola's chauffeur and pimp. Billy Luke owned the property until August 1930, when he sold it to John, Joe, and William Matties for $400.

The Matties brothers moved the restaurant on the corner to the back of the lot and joined the building to "Denver" Kate's old cabin. The two buildings were converted into a garage. The front of the lot was converted into a large garden. In the 1970's, a false-front building used for tourist shops was erected on the lot.

"JEW" FANNY

Fanny Wright, who went by the trade name of "Jew" Fanny, was from McKeesport, Pennsylvania. No one knows when she first came to Silverton. Fanny worked on Blair Street during the 1918 flu epidemic. According to "Leach" Zanoni, she acted as a nurse at the town pest house, which was located about a mile north of town. When itinerant miners were stricken with the disease, the county took them to the pest house, usually to die. Sometime after 1918 she moved to the tenderloin district of Telluride where she worked until 1923 when Telluride was "cleaned up." She returned to Silverton and rented the small crib in which Mayme Murphy was electrocuted. After a short while, she moved into the "Green House," next door to the north. In 1933, Nona Salfisberg worked as Fanny's hairdresser. She was often required to make house calls by the women on Blair Street to set their hair. She remembers doing Fanny's hair in the "Green House." She described Fanny's crib as follows:

> Fanny occupied the south half of the "Green House." The unit had a front room with two old-fashioned rocking chairs, one in front of the window. She had a red light which she would turn off when she had a customer. The bedroom was in the back with a double bed. The woodwork was spotless and everything was kept immaculately clean. She also rented the upstairs room directly above. I used to set her hair in a marcel wave. Fanny was a short, plumpish woman with a very pretty face. When I worked on her hair, she was probably in her early forties. She had a pimp named Hans Pavelich, a gambler. (His name was Marion Pavelich). Fanny kept him in the finest clothing. After she left Silverton, she married Hans.

Sometime in the mid-1930's, Fanny moved next door into the south wing of the National Hall. She occupied the ground floor facing Blair Street. Russ Kuhn relates the story of how a group of Silverton boys, just graduated from high school, wanted to give one of their friends a "treat." They approached "Jew" Fanny and told her their plan. The only problem was they could only come up with $1.60 of the required $2.00 fee. After a few minutes of serious negotiations, Fanny agreed on the $1.60 fee but she wanted them to know, "that she was losing money on the deal."

Mary Swanson recalls the day when Fanny came into her store to buy some cigarettes. Mary questioned her saying, "why do you buy these, you don't smoke?" Fanny replied: "I know, but I vant to be sociable."

In her later years, Fanny often kept one or two girls working for her. "Babe" also known as "Blonde Peggy," worked for her in the National Hall. "Babe" later moved to the Mikado.

Fanny could neither read or write. She had John Matties do much of her necessary correspondence. Over the years she sent money-orders to her relatives in Pennsylvania. She was buying an apartment building to take care of her in her old age. Instead of paying on her apartment, her relatives put the property in their own names and left her destitute. Because she could not write, she could not pay by check. If she had, she could have sued them for her savings.

Fanny was very popular in Silverton and held the distinction of being Silverton's last prostitute. She left in 1948. She moved to Denver and later Salida, Colorado, where she died a short time later.

Fig. 101   Blair Street between 11th and 12th streets, east side of street about 1947. Left to right: "Green House," Ludwig Vota's two cribs, Fattor's Tremount Saloon, Green Lantern (out of view), Zanoni-Pedroni Saloon and Tomaselli's Boarding House. Jim Bell Collection.

Fig. 102   "Corky" Scheer in front of Silverton's last county jail, now the Historical Society Museum. 1986. Allan Bird Photo.

Fig. 103 Photo of a Durango prostitute, about 1920. Andy Hanahan Photo.

Fig. 104 "Diamond Tooth" Leona's December, 1928 phone bill. Most of the calls were to brothels in Leadville, Telluride, and Durango. San Juan Co. Hist. Soc.

CHAPTER TWENTY-NINE

THE END
OF AN ERA

Silverton's red light district began to fade in the 1930's. By World War II, only a few women were still working on the "line." The death knell was rung when Edna Frecker managed to get on the city council. Edna was the daughter of Henry Frecker, the owner of the Grand Imperial Hotel. Henry Frecker bought the hotel in 1921 and changed the name from the Grand to the Imperial. Edna wanted to clean up the town. To quote Jim Hook, Sr., "she wanted no more whores, no more gambling, no more horses, no more dogs or cows running loose. She shut down Jack Gilheany." John Matties described her as, "a Carrie Nation type, she was a real bitch."

Edna Frecker succeeded in her efforts to close Silverton. "Jew" Fanny, the last prostitute, left in 1948. Also, about this time, the United States witnessed the beginning of the "sexual revolution."

"Jew" Fanny summed it up when she went for her mail for the last time. She told the postmaster, "You can't sell it when they're giving it away free."

THE END

LIST OF ILLUSTRATIONS

LIST OF ILLUSTRATIONS (Cont'd)

204